The Essential Guide to HR Management

*Critical Rules and Practical Tools to
Master the Fundamentals*

The Essential Guide to HR Management

Critical Rules and Practical Tools to Master the Fundamentals

Marcia Dennis

SkillPath® Publications

Editor: Bill Cowles

Layout and cover design: Barbara Hartzler

ISBN: 978-1-934589-95-3

Please note: The legal information provided in this book is of a general nature and cannot substitute for professional legal advice. Always seek the advice of competent counsel with any questions you may have regarding a legal issue. As legal advice must be tailored to the specific circumstances of each case, and laws are constantly changing, nothing provided herein should be used as a substitute for the advice of competent counsel.

Printed in the United States of America

Table of Contents

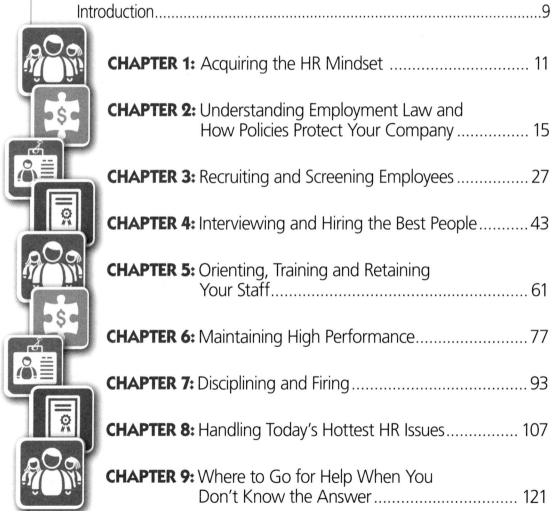

Introduction

Are you a newly appointed manager or supervisor handling "HR" responsibilities for the first time?

Are you feeling a little intimidated by how much there is to know?

Do you want to perform your HR duties with the knowledge and confidence that you're on solid legal ground?

This guide to the fundamentals of human resources management couldn't have come at a better time!

Today's managers and supervisors are being required to take on a wider and more complex range of HR issues than ever before. Undoubtedly, this is one of the most challenging functions of your job. It's also one of the most important.

To succeed, you need a greater understanding of the fundamentals of employment law: How to select, hire and manage staff effectively … how to deal with disciplinary and performance issues—and fire, when necessary … and other essential concepts you don't want to learn the hard way.

You cannot afford to tackle your new responsibilities without a solid foundation of the latest HR practices and processes and a clear understanding of the legal issues that influence your decisions. Your company is counting on you to do the right thing. Your subordinates are watching you, how you make decisions, your approach to performance issues—everything you do. Make even one single mistake and you put yourself and your company at risk. You also could damage—if not destroy—your professional reputation and your future career in management.

If you had the time and focus, you could do your own independent research nights and weekends and gradually learn what you need to know about HR. However, few managers can do that. But you can turn to this guide for help in developing indispensable skills and knowledge to ensure that you and your department are successful.

The Essential Guide to HR Management is a concise overview of the demanding HR issues managers and supervisors must deal with and the best-practice approaches for handling them—along with legally sound insight into the federal laws impacting your decisions so you'll know which rules apply and when.

This guide will help you:

- Understand and make sense of the volume of employment laws impacting your workforce
- Develop and enforce sound policies to protect your company
- Make informed decisions related to the ADA, EEOC, Affirmative Action—every regulation, no matter how complex
- Recruit and screen not just the *best* people—but the *right* people—without legal complications
- Conduct interviews using the latest techniques for identifying top candidates without risking legal liability
- Plan and implement thorough orientation sessions so every new hire comes on board successfully
- Implement the latest retention strategies
- Manage the day-to-day performance of your employees
- Discipline—and fire when necessary—legally and without fear
- And handle any HR situation and challenge with confidence

Good luck in handling the challenges ahead!

CHAPTER 1

Acquiring the HR Mindset

What does it take for managers and supervisors to succeed in the unfamiliar and often daunting role of human resources professional? It's not enough to have the right interviewing, counseling, hiring and other technical skills. You also need the right psychological and mental attitude—the right HR mindset.

As a manager just starting out in your new HR role, you probably won't understand what the right mindset is. One thing is for sure—you can't pick it up through study. You learn this skill through practice. And don't worry; you'll get plenty of field practice.

It's difficult to define, but it's easy to recognize managers who do have an HR mindset.

- They handle all their HR technical responsibilities fairly and objectively—hiring, disciplining and firing employees … conducting background checks … managing an employee's career development … training …conducting performance appraisals … all aspects of the employment process.

- They can deal with a wide variety of people of different educational levels, cultural heritages, religious practices, ages and work experience and show appropriate behavior at all times in all kinds of trying situations.

- They demonstrate first-class verbal and written communication skills.

- They confidently resolve conflicts—managers are in the middle of plenty of differences!

- They set and accomplish goals.

- They demonstrate a team attitude.

- They understand when certain issues need to be kept confidential.

How to Think Like HR

If you can adopt the right HR mindset and are willing to learn, you'll be successful. Let's look at the ingredients of that mindset more closely. The manager with an HR mindset:

Has dual focus. You'll need to consider the needs of both employees and management. Sometimes you'll need to make decisions to protect an employee and other times to protect your company. Employees at times may not understand this dual focus, and you may be criticized for it.

Is organized. Your files need to be organized and easily accessed should HR—or your company or attorney—need information on short notice. You're dealing with people's careers and futures. Losing an important piece of information or needing more time to find it is not acceptable.

Is able to multi-task. There is nothing predictable about handling human resources issues. Priorities, needs and expectations change rapidly. One day you may be counseling an employee about a drug problem. The next day you may be presenting a team excellence award. You need to be able to switch gears at a moment's notice and handle it all.

Shows discretion. As someone responsible for human resources management, you are the keeper of confidential information. You must ensure this information is handled properly and released only when appropriate. Knowing when to keep your mouth shut is absolutely vital—you can never share confidential information with others in or out of the organization who have no business knowing it.

Is consistent. You need to be predictably consistent. Employees need to know where you stand, what your expectations are, what your response will be. You can't afford to blame "bad days" for deciding or acting impulsively.

Sets a good example. Employees will be looking at you to set the emotional tone. If you're disgruntled, they will be too. If you break the rules sometimes, so will they.

Treats everyone fairly. It's your job to establish rules, convey them clearly to all employees and enforce them fairly.

Listens. A great deal of your job handling HR duties boils down to listening. By taking time to listen, you can avoid communication breakdowns and let employees know their voices will be heard and their opinions valued.

Is decisive. Don't be afraid to make the tough or unpopular calls.

Shows gratitude. Let employees know that you are grateful when they adhere to office policies and procedures. This will create an environment where they will want to continue doing what's right.

Shows integrity. You must be honest in all your dealings with the people you serve and those who serve you.

Is loyal. If your employees make an honest mistake once in a while and get in a jam with another manager, customer or vendor, support them. Never ridicule or punish them if they tried to do what was right.

Controls emotions. Don't ever allow your emotions to get in the way of treating employees fairly and equally. If you feel as if the situation will get heated, feel free to bring in a third party—like someone from HR—to mediate and defuse emotions.

Stays cool in a crisis. Sometimes an incident or accident may occur that gets everyone excited. It is your job to stay calm and cool, ensure as little damage as possible occurs and protect the interests of your employees and organization.

Is trustworthy. Demonstrate to employees that you can be trusted to protect them while being an advocate for the organization. It's no easy job.

Shows trust in employees. Don't micromanage or expect that employees will cheat the system. When your employees feel your trust for them, they will grow even more trustworthy and do an even better job.

Rate your "HR" qualities

How would your rate your qualities against those needed by an HR professional?

5 = the best   3 = average   1 = I need help

___ Fairness

___ Consistency

___ Well-organized

___ Ethics

___ Trustworthiness

___ Decisiveness

___ Integrity

___ Emotional control

Did you score a "5" all around? If not, there's still time to improve.

CHAPTER 2

Understanding Employment Law and How Policies Protect Your Company

In "the old days," managers and supervisors could comfortably do their job developing and motivating employees and leave employment law worries to the attorneys. Those days are over. You're on the front line—and on the hot seat. You've got to be legally savvy in everything you do—whether you're writing an advertisement to hire an employee, interviewing potential hires, dealing with tardiness problems or determining FMLA leave.

Are you confident you understand the latest employment laws governing how you manage employees on a day-to-day-basis? Are you sure your policies reflect the latest legislation and protect your company?

Understanding employment law—and the countless regulations, laws and federal and state decisions that impact your workplace—is a necessity. From the Family and Medical Leave Act to the Americans with Disabilities Act to the Fair Labor Standards Act, any manager who is unaware of the requirements of the law—and how to develop policies in relation to the law—is asking for trouble.

Learning on the job is not an option when you're facing governance by the Department of Labor, Equal Opportunity Commission, Internal Revenue Service and other government entities. Most certainly, should you be faced with an audit, investigation or even litigation, "I didn't know that" as a defense will not go far.

At-a-Glance Summary of Key Employment Laws

Employment law is a broad area encompassing all areas of the employee/employer relationship. It consists of thousands of federal and state statutes, local laws and judicial decisions.

Do you know what questions you can and can't ask during the application and interview process? Are you familiar with the pitfalls of conducting background checks? Do you know how to avoid discrimination charges and retaliation lawsuits? Can you develop policies without legal risk? What about handling excessive absenteeism, sexual harassment and other issues? Do you know how to properly terminate an employee? You need to learn how to handle any legal issue that comes your way.

A basic understanding of key employment laws is critical to avoiding costly lawsuits. Let's go over the basics every manager needs to be aware of to stay out of trouble:

Age Discrimination in Employment Act (ADEA) protects certain applicants and employees 40 years of age and older from discrimination on the basis of age in hiring, promotion, discharge, compensation or terms, conditions or privileges of employment. It prohibits discrimination on the basis of age in programs and activities receiving federal financial assistance.

Affirmative Action involves any program, policy or procedure an employer implements to correct past discrimination and prevent current and future discrimination in the workplace.

Americans with Disabilities Act (ADA) is a federal law that prohibits discrimination against qualified individuals with disabilities in job application procedures, hiring, firing, advancement, compensation, job training and other terms of employment. It applies to private employers, state and local governments, employment agencies and labor unions.

It covers employers with 15 or more employees. When an individual's disability creates a barrier to employment, the ADA requires employers to consider whether a "reasonable accommodation" could remove the barrier. This may involve making adjustments or modifications in the work, job application process, work environment, job structure, equipment, employment practices or the way that job duties are performed so that an individual can perform the essential functions of the job.

Civil Rights Act of 1964 is a federal statute enacted to guarantee the constitutional rights of individuals and prevent employment discrimination based on race, color, sex, religion, national origin or age.

Consolidated Omnibus Reconciliation Act (COBRA) of 1985 says that if an employee terminates employment with the company, the employee is entitled to continue participating in the company's group health plan for a prescribed period of time. This usually is 18 months. In certain circumstances—like an employee's divorce or death—the length of coverage may be longer for qualified dependents. COBRA is not extended to employees terminated for gross misconduct.

Employee Retirement Income Security Act (ERISA) of 1974 sets requirements for the provision and administration of employee benefit plans—including heath care benefits, profit sharing and pension plans.

Equal Pay Act (EPA) of 1963 is a federal law that prohibits employers from discriminating between male employees and female employees in terms of pay when they are performing jobs that are essentially the same or of comparable worth.

Fair Credit Reporting Act (FCRA) is a federal law that imposes strict rules on the ordering and use of consumer reports—including background checks, credit reports and other information gathered on applicants for employment.

Fair Labor Standards Act (FLSA) is a federal law that provides guidelines on employment status, child labor, minimum wage, overtime pay and record-keeping requirements.

Family and Medical Leave Act (FMLA) of 1993 allows employees who have met minimum service requirements (12 months employed by the company with 1,250 hours of service in the preceding 12 months) to take up to 12 weeks of unpaid leave per year for: A serious heath condition; to care for a family member with a serious health condition; the birth of a child; the placement of a child for adoption or foster care.

Health Insurance Portability and Accountability Act (HIPAA) of 1996 was enacted to make health insurance more "portable" from one employer to another. It provides new rights and protections for participants and beneficiaries in group health plans. It limits exclusions for preexisting conditions; prohibits discrimination against employees and dependents based on their health status; and allows a special opportunity to enroll in a new plan to individuals in certain circumstances.

Immigration Reform and Control Act (IRCA) of 1986 prohibits the employment of individuals who are not legally authorized to work in the United States or in an employment classification that they are not authorized to fill. It requires all employers to certify—using the I-9 form—within three days of employment the identity and eligibility to work of all employees hired. It also prohibits discrimination in employment-related matters on the basis of national origin or citizenship.

Occupational Safety and Health Act (OSHA) of 1970 sets forth standards that employers must comply with to provide working conditions for employees that are safe and free from health hazards. The law also requires employers to provide employees with protection against workplace hazards that could result in illness, injury or death and to communicate to employees the information on hazardous materials or chemicals they may be required to handle.

Sarbanes-Oxley Act of 2002 was enacted to increase accountability of corporations to their shareholders in the wake of recent accounting scandals. Two provisions of special interest to managers are the whistleblower protection provision and the 401(k) blackout notice provision.

Title VII of the Civil Rights Act of 1964, a provision of the Civil Rights Act of 1964, applies to employers with 15 or more employees. It provides protections to level the playing field by forcing employers to consider only objective, job-related criteria when making employment decisions. Title VII must be considered when reviewing applications and résumés, interviewing and testing candidates and considering employees for promotions, transfers or any other employment-related benefit or condition.

Q: Is discrimination ever legal?

A: Yes. In certain circumstances, an employer may have a legitimate business reason to hire an employee of a certain religion or gender. These are referred to as "bona fide occupational qualification (BFOQ) exceptions." For example, you may wish to hire a woman to watch over the women's dressing rooms in a department store.

Writing Legally Sound Policies to Protect Your Company

If you've been in management any length of time at all, you know one thing for sure: Employees will break the rules, misbehave and not follow your decisions. It is crucial that your employees know your company's and your department's official rules, procedures and regulations—so they can follow them. That's why documenting—in writing—how employees should conduct themselves is so important. Well-written policies will let employees know exactly what you expect of them. If you don't have important rules already in writing, now is the time to develop them.

What policies should be put in writing? Most companies have written policies on:

- At-will employment

- Pay procedures

- Benefits (including any paid vacation, sick leave, holidays and other forms of leave)

- Lunch and breaks

- Personal conduct on the job

- Vacation and sick leave

- Attendance and punctuality

- Sexual and other forms of harassment

- Equal employment opportunity

- Disciplinary procedures

- Termination

Q: I am concerned that if I don't have a written policy on every single thing, my employees will think a certain behavior is okay when it's not.

A: You can cover every workplace issue that comes up. The best approach is to make this clear to your employees by adding a statement in your handbook.

It's easy to feel daunted by the thought of writing clear policies that leave no room for misinterpretation. Here are some guidelines to help you formulate your ideas and write a well-constructed policy that is fair, consistent, complete and understandable by all.

Tips for writing effective policies:

- Do your homework. Read as much about the related legislation—if there is any—as you can.

- Benchmark what companies similar to yours are doing in the same area. Don't reinvent the wheel if you don't have to.

- Get input from team leaders and supervisors on the front line who may be responsible for enforcing the rules. You need their ownership.

- Get management support before you develop any policy. You'll need it when implementing it.

- Use the simplest words possible.

- Remember to write the policy for your entire workforce—not just a select group.

- Use positive language. Instead of telling employees what not to do, tell them what they can and should do.

- Don't write in legalese.

- Use the active—not passive—voice.

- Ask a small group of employees and front-line supervisors to review what you've written. Revise the policy if necessary.

- Have an employment law attorney review what you've written before you distribute it.

- Always aim for consistency and fairness.

- Keep the old version for legal backup if one policy replaces another.

- Plan how you will distribute the policy—in your employee handbook, on your intranet, during new employee orientation.

ALERT: Be sure to require employees to sign a form that says you have given them a copy of your policies—in case there is any question in the future. The acknowledgement, signed by the employee, can be as simple as: "I have received a copy of my company's employee manual."

Do you need to put your policies in writing?

Rate each question: 1 = never; 3 = sometimes; 5 = often

How often have you …

___ Been unsure if all employees are getting the same information and same "message" about the rules?

___ Wished you had something in writing to refer to when an employee misbehaves or commits an infraction?

___ Tried to remember if you ever discussed a certain rule with an employee?

___ Thought it would be a good idea to have employees sign a document saying they know the rules?

___ Worried an employee might file a lawsuit and wished you had something in writing to back you up in court?

___ Had an employee act confused about how to behave—like what dress is appropriate or whether or not they can take personal cell phone calls at work?

___ Felt employees needed more concrete guidance in certain areas—like deciding what the company will reimburse or not or phone coverage when people are at lunch or on vacation?

___ Been concerned things were slipping and you might not be in full compliance with laws like the FMLA or OSHA?

How did you do? Is it time get out your paper and pen and get busy?

Updating Policies to Reflect Your Changing Needs

When was the last time you reviewed your policies? Just because you've written and distributed a policy doesn't mean your job is done. The laws change rapidly. You must update your policies to keep them in line with new developments. When your policies don't reflect the latest changes, you will look bad—not only to your employees but also to a jury, should you end up before one.

Tips for updating your policies:

- Stay on top of changing laws. Think about how a change—even a minor one—affects your organization. In most cases, this requires an update to an existing policy. In other cases, it requires a brand new policy written specifically to address the legislation.
- Review your policies on a regular basis—at least once a year.
- Use a notification system to keep you alerted to changes in the laws.
- Inform employees immediately of any change in your policies and how the change will affect them or the work they do.

ALERT: You have the right to change your policies at any time. Review your policies regularly to identify policies you want to—or must—change.

Detecting Gaps in Your Policies That Put You at Risk

Don't let your organizational policies be the rope that hangs you in court.

- **Make sure your policies are consistent.** Inconsistency looks like discrimination to a judge. Your policies must treat everyone the same.
- **Do not create obligations you cannot keep.** Some courts interpret the language in policies as contracts that create binding obligations on employers. Avoid definitive language. Instead of saying "We will evaluate every employee annually" say "We will make every effort to conduct regular evaluations."
- **Reserve the right to change the policy at any time for any reason.** This will give you the freedom to eliminate a policy or add new policies.
- **Enforce your policies.** If you don't respond promptly when an employee fails to follow a policy you have established, your policies will be useless. You need to do everything within your power to reduce the number of potential claims—or at least be in a position to resolve them quickly—starting with consistent enforcement of your policies.

Minimizing Lawsuits

With numerous court decisions and rapidly changing employment legislation giving employees new protections in the workplace, it has become far too easy for employees to sue their employers. Many of these lawsuits could have been prevented, if the manager had only taken certain precautions designed to minimize the number of lawsuits and increase the company's defenses when such suits are brought about.

While you can't keep employees who feel they've been wronged from filing, you can take steps to reduce the number of lawsuits they do file. This could save you a fortune in time and money: Studies show that a company charged with wrongful termination could expect to pay legal costs up to $85,000 or more. And the toll on your productivity, morale and corporate image only adds to this amount.

First and foremost, you have to follow the laws. Simply being aware of the risks and seeking outside counsel when you are unsure how to proceed can prove a lot cheaper than suffering through a lawsuit.

Here are proactive steps you can take to minimize lawsuits:

- **Continually educate yourself.** Ignorance of the laws that impact your workplace is no defense. Become familiar with key employment laws and what you must do to comply. Staying on top of current laws will prepare you to create and establish the appropriate policies and procedures as well.

- **Get advice on the "gray areas" from an expert.** That may be the HR department in your company if you have one. If you don't, that may be an HR consultant. Or your company attorney.

- **Make sure all your employees know about your policies.** Your company's policies should be prominently posted in the workplace, distributed to employees and included in the employee handbook, if your company has one.

- **Train your employees.** Don't expect them to read the policies you issue or the employee handbook you give them at orientation. Train them on the most important areas—such as sexual harassment and negligent firing.

- **Stress the importance of compliance to employees.** And make sure they know the negative consequence of non-compliance.

- **Follow your company's discrimination and harassment policy.** An effective policy can prevent employee lawsuits or provide a compelling basis for their dismissal before trial. A policy will provide the steps employees must take should they have a complaint about harassment and discrimination so the problem can be addressed promptly and effectively before a lawsuit is filed. A policy will also provide you with a strong defense should the employee fail to follow the policy and your complaint procedure. It is to your advantage if you can claim you could have resolved the complaint internally had the employee filed a complaint.

- **Document every important meeting and decision.** Written documentation—covering every step in the employment process, from hiring to firing—is critically important and can't be over-stressed. You need to document decisions, meetings, problems, discussions, counseling—everything related to employee performance issues. Should you end up in court, your written documentation will be your greatest legal defense. The judge, the jury, your lawyer, the EEOC investigator—everyone will want to see what you have in writing. If it's not in writing, it didn't happen.

- **Do performance evaluations and make sure they are honest.** Too often, managers want to avoid confrontation and so downplay their criticisms of an employee's performance. As a result, the issue can fester and become even more difficult to resolve. To make matters worse, should the manager decide to formally discipline or terminate the employee, the employee can claim the manager made up the issue. Don't pat someone on the back for poorly performed work. You don't have to be punishing or overly negative. But it is important to discuss performance problems honestly so there are no surprises and employees may not be so quick to file a lawsuit.

- **Understand your at-will employment rights and preserve them.** At-will employment means that employers have the right to terminate employees at any time and for any reason not prohibited by law, with or without prior cause or notice. However, it is possible to forfeit this right—without realizing it. This may occur when, for example, you make statements in job interviews that lead employees to believe they have job security or that they may be terminated only for cause. Employment applications, offer letters and employee handbooks should contain a statement indicating employment with your company is "at-will"—and that either the employee or your company may terminate employment at any time and for any or no reason, with or without cause or prior notice.

Q: What are the most important things I can do to avoid lawsuits when hiring?

A: You should make every effort possible to avoid discrimination, respect your employees' right to privacy, follow the rules for hiring immigrants and avoid promising "job security."

Worksheet: Are you doing what you can to head off lawsuits?

Use this checklist to assess if your practices are legally safe and if you're doing what you can to sidestep lawsuits.

Check if true:

☐ I hire without even considering the person's age, race, gender or national origin.

☐ I consider a person's disability only in the context of job performance and if they can perform the job after reasonable accommodations are made.

☐ I have written job descriptions, including qualifications, for all positions.

☐ I inform employees of my performance standards.

☐ When performance is unsatisfactory, I give a reprimand in writing and the opportunity to correct the problem.

☐ I evaluate employees regularly, in writing.

☐ I am consistent and fair in all my interactions with employees.

☐ I do not tolerate discrimination.

☐ I terminate only for just cause.

☐ I look for red flags in job interviews and avoid hiring people likely to sue.

☐ I am responsible for making sure sexual harassment never occurs in my workplace.

If you are doing all these things on a regular basis, you're in a good position. If you were unable to check some items as true, work on improving your practices in these areas.

CHAPTER 3

Recruiting and Screening Employees

The words "I quit," when spoken by an employee you value, can be painful. Not only do you have to immediately cover that person's job duties, but you also have to start the long and painful process of finding a replacement. And you need to start fast. The longer you go shorthanded, the more productivity suffers.

You need a proven and efficient recruiting and screening process that you can activate immediately. This includes strong and up-to-date job descriptions, the know-how to write compelling advertisements and a good source of job candidates you can quickly tap into. Let's look at all these components.

Writing Job Descriptions

Starting a job search without a job description is like going on a hike blindfolded. You wind up going every which direction and end up nowhere. A job description is a written description of the duties, responsibilities, qualifications and reporting relationships of a particular job. It's important that it be written clearly and carefully because it defines what kind of person should be hired and the responsibilities and requirements of that person. And it provides a tool against which you can evaluate performance.

You should use the job description to write ads to run in newspapers, on on-line job boards and on your company's Web site. You also should use it when reviewing résumés, comparing candidates, developing job interview questions and screening.

A job description usually includes:

- **A job summary**—the position's key responsibilities in a brief one or two sentence statement

- **Qualifications**—such as specific skills, education, experience, certifications or licenses

- **Essential job functions**—the ADA seeks to make sure a person is not excluded from a job simply because the person cannot perform some marginal duties listed in the job duties. Essential job functions are those duties that are really the core of the job.

- **Nonessential job functions**—these are functions and duties that are preferred in a candidate, but not necessary

ALERT: A job description is considered a legal document. Vague and poorly-written job descriptions can be used against you in a wrongful termination lawsuit. Any reference to race, color, religion, age, sex, national origin or nationality, or physical or mental disability is illegal.

Tips for writing job descriptions:

- Update job descriptions regularly. Don't continually reuse a job description without thinking about your current needs and long-term objectives.

- Clarify the tasks the person will do before you think about the qualities required. The tasks will drive the qualities, attributes and characteristics needed in the employee.

- Avoid the risk of age discrimination by not including an upper limit on experience.

- Think about priorities in addition to the tasks and responsibilities that the job entails. What's most important in achieving success in the job?

- Make sure whatever credentials you deem necessary directly relate to the person's success on the job.

- Be careful not to create a job that is impossible to do or that few people could qualify for.

- Leave your options open.

Worksheet: Writing job descriptions

Think of the position you will be recruiting for next. Below write down the five skills or qualities most essential to this position in the order of importance—and use this priority to weed out unqualified applicants.

The position I will be filling:_____

The skills most essential in this position:

1.

2.

3.

4.

5.

Writing Job Advertisements

You want your job advertisements to pull the *best* candidates—not simply the *most* candidates. It will help to think of job advertisements as marketing tools. Your ad is directly competing against other ads. So you must do everything you can to draw the best candidates and get them excited about the opportunity to work for your company—not drive them away. Having a good job description in hand will save time when writing ads. You can refer to it for the main points you want to make in the ad instead of trying to figure out what to say from scratch.

Tips for writing advertisements for the newspaper or on-line:

- **Be specific.** Write the ad to attract the cream of the crop. Give enough information about whom and what you are looking for so unqualified applicants will be discouraged from applying.

- **Be clear.** Make sure the job duties, qualifications and requirements of the job are clearly stated—and not buried in corporate gobbledygook.

- **Be honest.** If the person must have an MBA in Asian Art, state that clearly.

- **Start with a heading that will grab the candidate's attention.** If you have a position for a direct mail specialist, for example, write the heading so it stands out from all the other jobs—like Response-driven Direct Mail Specialist Needed

- **Realistically describe the working environment**—fun, casual, corporate, etc.

- **Provide the hours, pay range and benefits.** (Hint: If you list the pay range, you will have to screen fewer résumés.)

- **Make it challenging to apply.** For example, require a cover letter that addresses a major challenge of the job and the applicant's experience in handling similar situations. People who aren't really interested won't go to the trouble of writing the cover letter.

- **Avoid discriminatory language.** It's against the law to discriminate against applicants of a particular gender, age or other protected class. It makes your company look bad. And many newspapers won't accept the ad. For example, say "high-energy" instead of "young" … "salesperson" instead of "salesman" … or "excellent source of secondary income for retired persons" instead of "retired persons preferred."

If your company offers any of these benefits or perks, be sure to list them—it's a great way to snag top talent:

- Salary or pay that exceeds the industry standard
- Training provided—list the skills the employee will learn
- Potential for pay raises when new skills are mastered
- Tuition reimbursement
- A company car
- Medical and dental insurance
- A flexible work schedule
- Opportunity to telecommute
- Bonuses
- A scheduled pay raise
- Advancement opportunities
- On-site cafeteria, health club, day care
- 401(k) plan

Here is an example of a job posting that was created from a job description.

> ### Response-driven Direct Mail Specialist Needed
>
> *Company ABC, an award-winning advertising agency serving a global market, seeks a motivated, self-starting Direct Mail Specialist to develop direct marketing strategy and materials and support the overall marketing function. The successful candidate will have a degree in marketing and at least 5 years of experience in marketing by mail. The successful candidate will have initiative, be creative, have a working knowledge of postal regulations and be able to write direct mail copy. Company ABC offers a competitive salary and a generous benefits package. Please send résumé with salary requirements to: HRDepartment@ABCCompany.com.*

> **Q:** The job opening I have is best filled by someone over 50. I can't say this in the ad—what can I say to discourage younger applicants?
>
> **A:** It may take just a few words to get the idea across—legally. Try using the words "reliable" … "responsible" … "experienced."

Finding Qualified Applicants

Finding talented, skilled and hardworking employees isn't easy. The most successful managers are always on the prowl. It takes time, patience and persistence. One thing is for sure—in most cases, they aren't going to be knocking at your door. If the person you are seeking is not currently a member of your staff, where will you find them? What type of advertising will you do? You have to have a well-defined recruitment plan to fill the pipeline.

Here are some sources of leads. Which ones might work for you?

Look inside your company:

- **Check out internal candidates.** Could an existing employee in another area fill the position? Someone who is ready for a promotion? You already know the pros and cons of such a person so there's less hiring risk. And the person knows your organization which should reduce the learning curve. It's also good for other employees to see that there may be opportunities to advance in your organization.

Look outside your company:

- **Post the job on your Web site.** This is a good way to attract job seekers who are aware of your organization and interested in working there.

- **Advertise in your newspaper.**

- **Uses the state Employment Service**—sometimes called Job Service, Public Employment, Unemployment Bureau, or Employment Security Agency.

- **Use employment agencies.** Some specialize in finding industry- or skill-specific employees. Most provide screening services including background checks and aptitude tests—although you can expect to pay a considerable fee for these services.

- **Use headhunters.** A headhunter may be the right route to take for certain executive-level jobs or if you don't have time to handle the search yourself and need outside help, though you'll have to pay a sizeable fee.

- **Look to your competition.** Employees who work for your competitors may not be actively looking, but may respond if you provide them with a better opportunity. Be sure to check with your lawyer in case non-compete agreements are a barrier.

- **Use university career centers.** Recent graduates are often overlooked because they lack work experience. The flip side is that they are moldable and can be trained to fit your company and requirements.

- **Post Help Wanted signs on your storefront**. They're free and no-risk, although they may attract many applicants who are unqualified.

Advertise on-line on:

- **On-line job sites.** The Web contains many sites where you can post a job—such as Monster.com and CareerBuilder.com.

- **On-line classified sections from major newspapers.** This channel can provide the largest pool of prospective employees.

- **Professional association Web sites.**

Get referrals:

- **Ask friends, family and current employees for recommendations.** Your chance of a good hire increase when it's someone who's been highly recommended by a person you trust. If you don't have a formal process for regularly soliciting referrals from your employees, start one.

- **Reward employees for referring job candidates.** Give a bonus, if you can, when the candidate is actually hired. Instruct your employees on what to tell interested people about your company, benefits, work environment, promotion opportunities and other perks. You can even ask your employees what appeals to them about your company and use their points.

Do you really need to hire an employee? Or could you use:

- **Interns.** Provided through colleges and universities, these include students who work for you part-time or even for free for the opportunity to learn about your business and get work experience in the real world.

- **Temporary help services.** Workers supplied by a temporary service firm are available immediately—even the same day. The rate paid to a temporary service firm is often higher than you would pay an employee, but you save the costs of recruiting, benefits, training and overtime. Rule of thumb: If you need a temporary worker for more than six months, consider hiring a full-time employee.

Q: Usually I find employees through word-of-mouth. Do I have to advertise the positions anyway?

A: No—unless you are in federal, state or local government, and then you do. However, you may wish to advertise the position anyway. You may bring in more applicants to choose from, you won't get the reputation of hiring "friends" or playing favorites and you may help avoid the appearance of discrimination— especially if your word-of-mouth advertising is limited to those of a certain race, religion or ethnic background.

Worksheet: Finding great employees

Your administrative assistant resigns. You need to begin recruiting a replacement immediately. How will you create a pool of applicants? For each recruitment method, mark in the appropriate box how important the method is for this particular job.

How important is this?

	Not important	Somewhat	Very
Newspaper ad	☐ Not important	☐ Somewhat	☐ Very
On-line job board	☐ Not important	☐ Somewhat	☐ Very
Professional association Web site	☐ Not important	☐ Somewhat	☐ Very
Referrals	☐ Not important	☐ Somewhat	☐ Very
Job posting in lunch room	☐ Not important	☐ Somewhat	☐ Very
Help Wanted sign	☐ Not important	☐ Somewhat	☐ Very
Headhunter	☐ Not important	☐ Somewhat	☐ Very
Career center at university	☐ Not important	☐ Somewhat	☐ Very
Employment agency	☐ Not important	☐ Somewhat	☐ Very

Reviewing Résumés

Don't be surprised if some of the jobs you advertise turn out a flood of responses—certain jobs may bring in hundreds of applications. The fact is, most of these applicants will be unqualified. So—unless you want to spend hours reviewing résumés and weeding out these "no's"—you need to be able to screen résumés quickly and accurately to pick out the gems.

You can no longer rely on traditional techniques when screening résumés. The type of stationery, envelope and "look" of the cover letter are not as important as they once were. Today many applications are sent electronically from job boards and lose their formatting in the process anyway. However, still important are proper spelling and grammar, a résumé that delivers a candidate's skills in a scannable format, and an overall flawless presentation.

If you have created a job description for the position, you're ahead of the résumé-reviewing game. You can use the job description to create an "ideal candidate profile"—listing the most important skills, experience, education and other factors.

How to review a résumé in 30 seconds:

- **Read the cover letter.** Look for proper spelling and punctuation, an overall air of quality and the applicant's attention to detail. If there's no cover letter, you may consider putting the application in the rejection file. Not always, but usually, the people who fail to include a cover letter are unqualified.

- **Skim the résumé.** Look for easy-to-find "must-have" qualifications—like a college degree or experience with certain software.

- **Read the "objective" the candidate wrote.** If it is not customized to your position, consider dumping the résumé.

- **Read the summary of qualifications and experience.** If the candidate has customized this section to match the details of your job, then consider putting the résumé in the "possibility" file.

- **Read the candidate's experience, contributions and recent employers.** Unless something looks terribly wrong here—like unexplained gaps in employment, several short stints at jobs or a major career direction change—then keep the résumé for more review.

Tip: The more résumés you review, the better you'll get at screening them. With practice, you can conduct this part of the hiring process fairly quickly.

Worksheet: Reviewing résumés

The next time you have a stack of résumés to review—and not a lot of time—don't get stressed. Use this checklist to remind you of what's important and speed through the process.

☐ The applicant's "objective" on their résumé matches your job.

☐ A summary statement of qualifications and experience has been customized to your job.

☐ Basic required qualifications—like a college degree—are there.

☐ Recent employers, experience, accomplishments, and contributions have been included.

☐ Proper spelling and grammar is evident throughout. Attention to detail is apparent— for example, if you required a cover letter, is there one?

☐ Red flags—such as employment gaps, signs of decreasing responsibility and evidence a career has plateaued—have been noted.

Conducting Background Checks

Before making a hiring decision, you may want to check into applicants' backgrounds to make sure they are who they say they are and have done the things they say they've done. You can no longer make a few phone calls to the references candidates provide and feel like you've got a good handle on their background. You may need more information—sometimes a lot more—to clear up any doubts about the person. You may want to know about a person's past employment, any criminal background and whether they've filed workers' comp claims. You also may wish to verify their education and whether or not they actually have the degrees or licenses they say they do.

Background checks are becoming more important with the increase in security concerns, corporate scandals and workplace violence. Some of the reasons to conduct background checks include to:

- **Avoid negligent hiring lawsuits.** If you hire an employee who does something to hurt someone else, you as the employer could be liable. Failure to carefully check an employee's background could cost your company a lot and tarnish your reputation as a manager.

- **Comply with laws requiring background checks.** The federal government requires background checks for certain jobs, often as part of security clearance investigations. Certain state and federal laws require employers to conduct background checks when jobs require people to work with children or the sick, disabled or elderly.

- **Verify the true identities of employees.** In a world of tightening security, identities of employees may need to be verified by employers—especially illegal immigrants.

- **Avoid scandals.** In the aftermath of Enron, the personal and professional lives of corporate executives, officers and directors are being more closely scrutinized.

- **Detect false or inflated information on résumés.** This problem is increasing—studies show 30% or more of job applications and résumés include lies.

Employment background checks are generally legal. But you don't have unlimited access to an applicant's information. And applicants have a right to privacy in certain areas. If you pry into areas you shouldn't, you could get sued. That's why you need to know your limits within the law.

Laws regulating background checks include the Fair Credit Reporting Act (FCRA) which protects the privacy of a person's consumer reports. It imposes strict rules on how you order and use consumer reports which include background checks, credit reports and other information gathered on potential employees in the pre-employment stage. Additional federal laws contain privacy provisions that restrict access to public school and medical records, as well as other records maintained by government agencies. And various state laws may deal with the access to public and personal information.

When you think of "background checks" you may automatically think this means checking into a person's criminal background. It could. But typically, a background check involves a lot more.

Depending on the laws that apply, a background check may include verification of:

- Driving record
- Social security number
- Bankruptcy
- Property ownership
- Past employers
- Vehicle registration
- Education records
- Character references
- Personal references
- Military records
- Credit report
- Court records
- State licensing records
- Incarceration records
- Criminal records
- Workers' compensation
- Sex offender registry

Tips for safely conducting background checks:

1. **Be aware of certain rules** that apply to certain types of information:

   - **Education records.** These records—including transcripts, recommendations, discipline records and financial information—are confidential. However, a school may release information which includes name, address, dates of attendance, degrees earned and activities if the student gives written permission.

   - **Credit reports.** You need the applicant's written consent to check credit reports. Many employers automatically ask for this on the application form.

   - **Bankruptcies.** While bankruptcies are public record, you cannot discriminate against applicants because they have filed for bankruptcy.

   - **Criminal records.** The law varies depending on the state, so be sure to consult with a lawyer before probing into someone's criminal past.

   - **Workers' compensation records.** You may consider information contained in the public record from a workers' compensation appeal in making a job decision if the applicant's injury could interfere with his or her ability to perform the job.

   - **Military records.** These are confidential. However, the military may release name, rank, salary, duty assignments, awards and duty status.

   - **Medical records.** These are confidential in many states unless the applicant gives specific permission for the release of them.

2. **Limit background checks only to information that relates to the job.** If you are hiring a store manager who may have access to large amounts of money, then a criminal background check may be a good idea. If you're hiring a receptionist, it may not.

3. **Get the applicant's permission in writing.** If the applicant refuses, then you have the legal right not to hire the person on that basis.

4. **Use common sense.** Don't go overboard checking every single detail about someone.

Q: Can I just cut to the chase and ask job applicants if they have an arrest record?

A: No—this can be a subtle form of discrimination. Besides, rarely is there a good reason to reject an applicant based on an arrest record. A conviction, however, is another story. Generally, you may inquire about an applicant's conviction record if it's a job-related concern—for example, you don't want to hire an applicant who has been convicted of drunk driving to drive a school bus.

Q: I suspect an applicant did not earn the degree he says he did. Do I have a right to see his academic records?

A: Federal law prohibits schools that receive federal funds to release academic records without the student's permission. You must ask the applicant to sign a written release acknowledging your right to obtain them.

Worksheet: What type of background check is necessary?

It depends on the employee and the job. Keeping in mind you want to limit background checks to only the information that relates to the job, decide what would be prudent for the positions below.

Position	Type of background check needed
Security guard	
Telemarketer	
Law enforcement	
Child care provider	
Customer service rep	
Home health care aide	
Retail—handles cash	

Checking References

Reference checking is usually done at the end or near the end of the interview process. It's a good idea to check references. Too many job applicants falsify their information on applications and résumés or leave information out. By talking to past employers, you can verify their background and learn a lot about the person that you didn't know.

When you reach the stage where you are serious about a candidate, ask the candidate to give you the name and contact information of one reference for every job worked. Before you start calling, understand that many employers concerned with privacy lawsuits now refuse to offer more than dates of employment, salary history and job title. Some employers have policies requiring managers to only confirm dates of employment, salary and other limited information.

How can you get beyond the screen? Get the applicant to sign a waiver permitting you to ask past employers detailed information about their employment. Offer to fax the signed waiver over to the employers you are checking references with—it may ease their fears about being sued by the employee.

Once you get a past employer on the phone, ask probing questions like these:

- What was (name's) position and job responsibilities?
- Did (name) miss much work? Arrive late very often?
- Did (name) get along well with others?
- How did (name) handle conflict? Pressure? Stress?
- What were (name's) strengths? Weaknesses? Biggest accomplishments?
- If I read the description of the job we're considering (name) for, could you tell me if you think (name) would be a good fit?
- Can you tell me anything else about (name) that I should know?

Tips for checking references:

- Only do checks on candidates you are serious about. You'll save time and avoid unnecessary risk.

- Be sure to tell the applicant you will be calling the references provided.

- Prepare your questions in advance. Don't wing it—you may waste the past employer's time and end up without the information you really need.

- Ask open-ended questions—not questions the former employer can answer "no" or "yes" to.

- Be specific. If you have an area of concern—like the person's attitude or record of attendance—ask about it.

- If you are checking references on several employees, ask the same questions of each former employer to be fair.

Q: Should I rely on a prospective employee's word when trying to verify salary information? Or try verifying it with a past employer?

A: The best way to verify salary is by requesting to see a current paycheck stub.

CHAPTER 4

Interviewing and Hiring the Best People

Hiring employees is a big part of a manager's job. And the job interview, if conducted skillfully, is a powerful tool for bringing the best people into your organization. By asking the right questions you can differentiate between two seemingly equal candidates, get a feel for whether or not a candidate would fit into your culture and identify key qualities and skills that could support your efforts.

Interviewing Ground Rules

Before you get started, you need to know the interviewing ground rules:

- **Schedule interviews as soon as possible after receiving applications.** You don't want the best candidate to take another job and slip away.

- **Allow ample time for each interview.** Don't take calls or allow interruptions or distractions. Don't keep the candidate waiting.

- **Do your homework.** Carefully review the candidate's résumé and any other materials before the interview.

- **Develop a list of questions in advance** based on the position and the type of person you are looking for.

- **Ask open-ended questions** that will encourage the candidate to talk openly. In other words, don't ask questions that can be answered "yes" or "no."

- **Ask the same questions of every applicant.** This will ensure consistency and fairness and enable you to control the conversation. It also will reduce the opportunity to ask unplanned questions that are illegal.

- **Be respectful.** Make applicants feel welcomed by offering them coffee or a soft drink.

- **Dress and act professionally.** Model the behavior you would expect of the employee.

Asking Legally Safe Questions

Interviewing is subject to both state and federal laws which define employment discrimination in all aspects of employment. Together, these laws forbid you to discriminate in hiring on the basis of sex, age, race, national origin, religion, physical disability or veteran status. These are called protected classes and questions about any aspect of these topics during an interview are illegal.

Asking the wrong interview questions can lead to discrimination or wrongful-discharge lawsuits, won or lost based on statements made during the interview process. At any time, you or your company could be accused of asking improper interview questions or making statements or comments that reflect discrimination and bias. You could also be accused of making promises during an interview that can be interpreted as binding contracts. Recognizing potential danger areas is the best way to avoid saying the wrong thing during an interview.

Do NOT:

- Ask questions related to: Age, race, ethnicity, color, gender, sex, country of national origin, birthplace, religion, disability, marital or family status or pregnancy.
- Make statements that suggest you are creating a contract of employment. For example avoid words like: "Permanent," "long-term" or "job security."

Questions you may NOT ask:

- Who takes care of your children while you work?
- What are the ages of your children?
- What year did you graduate from high school?
- Do you think you can take directions from a younger boss?
- Are you a U.S. citizen?
- Where does your wife work?
- Where did you grow up?
- Do you think you'd have any problem working for a female boss?
- Many of the employees in this department are older than you. Is that a problem?
- Do you plan to start a family?
- When do you hope to retire?
- How's your health? Have you suffered serious illnesses recently?
- Is there any health-related reason why you could not perform this job?
- At your last job, how many days were you absent because of illness?
- Do you take any prescription medications?
- Do you have a drug or alcohol problem?
- Do you rent or own your home?

Questions you MAY ask:

- Are you authorized to work in the U.S?
- Do you speak any languages fluently?
- What is your current phone number and address?
- What days are you available to work?
- Do you belong to any association that is relevant to our industry?
- Are you over the age of 18?
- What long-term career goals have you set?
- Can you travel?
- Are you available to work overtime?
- What made you decide to apply for a job at our company?
- Can you describe your last job?
- Why did you leave your last job?
- If we call your previous employer, what would they say about you?
- What kind of work environment do you feel most comfortable in?
- We're seeking flexible people—is that how you'd describe yourself?

Q: What if a candidate brings up an "illegal" topic—like child care?

A: If an applicant volunteers information—for example if someone tells you he will have to leave by 3 p.m. because he has to pick up his children from school—then you can respond to the question.

Q: If a candidate has an obvious disability, can I ask how it will affect how they perform the job?

A: The ADA forbids you to ask if an applicant has a disability. If it is obvious the applicant does or if the applicant volunteers this information, you may ask whether the applicant will need an accommodation to do the job.

Probing Deeper With Behavior-based Questions

One of the biggest mistakes managers make when interviewing is asking only factual questions—closed questions a candidate can answer with "yes," "no" or a fact or date and which reveal nothing about the real person. For example: "When did you join your last employer?" or "How long were you in the position?"

Open-ended questions will produce a better result—questions like "Tell me about your management style" or "Describe a time when you had to expand your comfort zone." Such questions are the basis of behavioral interviewing—an interviewing technique that allows you to focus on likely future performance based on past behavior.

In a behavioral interview, the interviewer focuses on specific situations and examples, not hypothetical situations. The questions asked require the candidates to describe how they actually acted in specific work situations in their past. Behavioral interviews are an effective way to identify candidates who have the behavioral traits and characteristics that you have determined as necessary for performing and succeeding in a particular job. By asking behaviorally based questions, you can gain valuable insight into how the candidate may respond to issues and problems faced in your workplace.

Tips for conducting a behavior-based interview:

- Familiarize yourself thoroughly with the candidate's résumé, application, cover letter and other submitted materials.

- Have a good idea of what the candidate might bring to the position, if hired.

- Identify the experiences, behaviors, knowledge, skills and abilities that you have determined are necessary for success in the position—like initiative, teamwork, ability to travel and confidence.

- Pay close attention to the candidate's responses. How recent are the examples? How effective was the person's behavior in the story? Look for concrete, verifiable evidence.

- Consider giving each candidate the list of interview questions in advance.

- Ask short and simple questions.

- Keep your comments neutral.

- If the candidate becomes silent after you ask a question, re-assure the candidate and re-phrase the question.

- Take notes. You need to be able to remember specific responses to make the best hiring decisions.

- Ask a variety of types of questions—situational, behavioral and job-knowledge-based, for example.

Sample behavior-based interview questions:

- Describe a situation in which you were able to use negotiation to get what you needed.

- Describe a time when you were faced with a difficult deadline situation that demonstrated your stress management skills.

- Tell me about a specific time when you used creativity to solve a problem.

- Tell me about a situation in which you were expected to speak before a large group.

- Discuss the last document you were required to write.

- Tell me about the last time you had too many things due at the same time and had to prioritize your work.

- How do you respond in situations when you're expected to make a decision on the spot?

- How would you describe your style when dealing with conflict?

- What's the toughest decision you had to make at your last job? Tell me about the process you used to make it.

Q: When conducting behavioral interviews, do I still need to ask every applicant the same questions to prevent the impression of bias?

A: Yes. It is not uncommon for applicants to complain about disparate treatment when being interviewed. You must do everything possible to ensure you treat all applicants equally.

Worksheet: Behavioral interviewing

Think about an upcoming interview you will be conducting. What five behaviorally-based questions could you ask that would help reveal the real applicant? Write them down here.

Position: _____

Question #1 _____

_____

Question #2 _____

_____

Question #3 _____

_____

Question #4 _____

_____

Question #5 _____

_____

Conducting Pre-employment Screening Tests

More and more companies are using pre-employment testing to evaluate skills, attitudes, knowledge and abilities before hiring employees. A pre-employment test is a standardized and objective tool for determining if an applicant is right for a particular position—and for comparing one job candidate to another to make the hiring decision.

If used correctly—and legally—pre-employment tests can help you screen out people who are not suitable for the job and avoid costly hiring mistakes. However, the downside is that state and federal laws impose many restrictions on what you can do. **To avoid risks, you should only use tests designed to predict a worker's actual ability to do the job.**

Different types of testing include:

- **Skills tests.** These include such tests as typing and math tests and are usually legal if you test skills necessary for the employee to perform the job.

- **Aptitude, psychological and personality tests.** Be careful with these tests. Their ability to predict an employee's future conduct is still questioned. Plus, many of these tests include questions that are personal and could lead to charges of discrimination and invasion of privacy.

- **Lie detector tests.** Federal law prohibits private employers from requiring employees to take lie detector tests, with some exceptions. (For example, if you're hiring a security guard, a lie detector test may be acceptable.) Nor can you use the results of such tests to make employment decisions. In those cases where you are allowed to require lie detector tests, you must be careful they aren't discriminatory or violate a person's privacy.

- **Medical tests.** You may not require a job candidate to take a medical test. However, once the person is hired, you can require a medical exam to prove if an employee is physically or mentally fit or unfit to do the job.

- **Drug testing.** The laws on drug testing vary from state to state. In general, courts have consistently upheld the legality of requiring a pre-employment drug test as a condition of employment. It is a best practice to obtain consent and clearly indicate drug testing is a requirement for employment.

All pre-employment assessment tools have one thing in common: They must comply with applicable laws. Specifically, they must comply with standards set by the Equal Employment Opportunity Commission. Think for a moment about the test you're considering using.

Answer the following questions—based on legal guidelines of the EEOC—to determine if a pre-employment test is legally safe:

- Does it measure skills or work behavior important to the performance of the specific job you're considering the applicant for?

- Will you administer it to all candidates for the same job in a fair and uniform manner?

- Are you certain the tests will not have a discriminatory impact against an applicant of any race, religion, sex or ethnic group?

- Is the test validated—is there a demonstrated correlation between the individual's performance on the test and future performance on the job?

- Will the standard used to score the test be applied consistently?

If you can answer "yes" to each of the above questions, it may be safe to assume the test you are about to use is legal and fair.

Q: When exactly in the interview process should I introduce testing?

A: This can vary. You may wish to have applicants take the test right after they complete the job application and before the interview to reduce the time you spend interviewing. Or you may wish to make the test the last step in the selection process. Either way, you need to be consistent.

ALERT: Avoid discriminating against people protected by the ADA. The tests you use must accurately measure their skills, not their abilities. Do not use tests that reveal anything about a mental impairment or psychological condition.

Worksheet: Pre-employment testing

Could pre-employment testing be valuable in your hiring decision making? Check the statements that are true.

☐ I rely mostly on the interview, résumé, reference checks and my gut feeling when making hiring decisions.

☐ It seems too many new employees fail to perform once they're on the job.

☐ I have turnover problems. We need to stabilize our workforce and find employees who are committed.

☐ We're going through a growth period and need to hire a lot of employees quickly.

☐ The new employees I bring on board often leave within six months.

If the answer is "yes" to even one, you should consider administering personnel testing during the hiring process.

Making the Hiring Decision

After completing the often long process of interviewing candidates, you are left with one big and important decision—who to offer the job to. Peter Drucker, renowned management consultant, wrote that only one-third of hiring decisions are successful. Interviews often last 30-60 minutes, but more often than not, interviewers make the hiring decision within the first five minutes. You can greatly reduce the odds of making a mistake at this critical juncture by having a formal, deliberate process in place to ensure the best person is hired.

Tips for making the hiring decision:

- Ask yourself if you have enough information to make a decision. If you don't, schedule another interview.

- Don't rely totally on your gut. Take time to consider the candidate's true skills, ability and personality.

- Don't focus solely on the technical skills required by the job. Other skills are just as important—like the ability to work with others, plan, negotiate, self-manage and work on a team.

- Don't hire people who are competent but not motivated to do the job. Uncovering whether a person is motivated to do the job may take longer, but it is time well spent.

- Don't hire people who can do certain parts of the job well, but not the whole job. It's easy to be wowed by a person who has enormous experience in one area, but you may end up doing more training for the other parts of the job than you anticipated.

- Don't overlook hiring great people who got nervous during the interview and so didn't come across well. Not everyone makes a good first impression. Bring those people back and interview them again in a more relaxing setting.

- Get another opinion: Invite at least one other co-worker to be involved in the hiring process if possible. This will give you a valuable second opinion and reduce the likelihood that you are "wowed" by someone who makes an outstanding first impression. You may consider enlisting an employee with hands-on knowledge of the position and what it takes to succeed.

- Narrow the pool of candidates down to a few. Ask each of them back for a second interview. During this interview, you can probe in more depth into some of the areas you originally discussed and get answers to any unanswered questions you may have. You also can ask the candidates about their ideas for the position and how they might handle the job.

Q: I can't seem to get a straight answer when interviewing certain applicants. What can I do when they seem evasive?

A: Keep digging. You may need to ask three or more similar questions to get to the truth.

Worksheet: Comparing candidates

Is your head spinning after interviewing candidate after candidate? This is precisely why you need to follow a structured process for comparing candidates. Fill out this form the next time you are comparing candidates before the final decision.

Job Specifications	Candidate 1	Candidate 2	Candidate 3
Experience			
Education			
Compatibility			
Other factors			

Making the Job Offer

After you've held interviews, conducted background checks, checked references, tested and made your hiring decision, you're ready to make the job offer. This should be a positive experience. Think of it as an opportunity to welcome the employee to your company, express what a great addition they will be and launch a solid working relationship between the two of you.

At the same time, this is a situation where you could get into legal trouble down the road if you're not careful. The biggest risk you face is unintentionally making statements the potential employee could misconstrue as a written contract. Remember, employment-at-will laws give you wide latitude in firing employees and you wouldn't want to jeopardize that by suggesting job security to an employee. This could make it difficult to fire the employee if you wanted to.

Do NOT promise:

- "Permanent employment"

- "Long-term security"

- "You can stay here and grow with us"

- "There are no layoffs here"

- "A long and rewarding career"

- "We'll pay part of your moving expenses now and the remainder after one year"

Tips for making the job offer:

- **Act quickly.** Make the offer as soon as possible. If you delay, your best applicant could end up at your competitor's.

- **Make the offer in person, over the phone or in writing.** Tip: If you make it over the phone, you'll get a response more quickly.

- **Double-check the salary or pay rate the candidate expects** before making the offer. You don't want to look foolish by offering $30,000 to a candidate currently making $45,000.

- **Cover the basics when making the offer.** These include the position you are offering, where the employee will work, the working hours, salary, benefits, starting date and the date the employee must accept by.

- **Sell the person on the job.** Go over the key benefits of accepting the job and working at your company. Mention bonus programs, training opportunities, advancement possibilities and any other aspects of employment that will convince the applicant to say yes.

- **Stay in touch after the employee accepts.** Avoid buyer's remorse. Send relevant information to the new hire, keep in touch by e-mail or phone and ask if there is anything else you can do to ensure their successful start.

- **Be prepared to negotiate the offer**—in case the employee rejects your initial offer. Can you offer more money? Additional vacation? Make sure your follow-up offer is too good to pass up.

- **Clear up any tests**—like a drug test or medical exam—the employee must take before starting.

Be sure to send a follow-up letter (not to the person's current place of employment) that summarizes the position, where the person will be located, the hours, salary, benefits, starting date and any additional information the candidate needs to bring the first day. Also establish a date you expect a response from the applicant.

> **Q:** If an applicant is reluctant to accept my job offer, how far should I go when trying to convince him or her to say yes?
>
> **A:** Be willing to give a little by throwing in a few perks. But be careful about agreeing to anything big—like a considerably higher salary. This can have a negative impact on your organization's pay scale. Plus, persuading an applicant with serious reservations from the start may backfire on you later.

Before making the final offer—make sure you've covered all the bases:

- Have you scheduled and held interviews with any interested internal candidates and informed those who were not selected?

- Have you developed a job description and thought through the key requirements of the job and the characteristics, education and experience you seek in a candidate?

- Have you posted the position internally?

- Have you advertised the position?

- Have you screened résumés against the qualifications and criteria you established?

- Did candidates complete your company's job application when they arrived for their interview?

- Did you give each candidate the job description to review?

- Did you carefully describe your organization and your needs during the interviews?

- Did you include the appropriate people in the second interviews—for example, potential co-workers and HR?

- Did you schedule additional interviews, if necessary?

- If you conducted testing, did all the candidates complete the same tests?

- Did you check the references of the people you were considering offering the position to?

- Did you stay in contact with your top candidates throughout the process?

- Did you reach a decision about whom to hire after consulting with all the staff who were involved and HR?

- Did you talk with the chosen candidate to gauge his or her interest in the position?

- Did you tell the candidate a non-compete must be signed, if required by your company?

TIP: Remember, a wrong hiring decision can make your life miserable. Don't saddle yourself with the wrong people—it's too hard to get rid of them. Put the time, effort and energy into hiring the right person the first time.

Worksheet: Negotiating the job offer

Think about an applicant who rejected your job offer. What else could you have added to the offer to sweeten the pot? Check the items that may have been negotiable:

Position:_____

- ☐ Job title
- ☐ Who they report to
- ☐ Start date
- ☐ Salary/bonus/commissions
- ☐ Signing bonus
- ☐ Profit sharing/stock options
- ☐ Health/dental/vision insurance
- ☐ Life insurance/accidental death
- ☐ Short-term/long-term disability
- ☐ Vacation
- ☐ Holidays
- ☐ Sick/personal days
- ☐ Comp time/overtime
- ☐ 401(k) match
- ☐ Pension
- ☐ Tuition reimbursement
- ☐ Training
- ☐ Relocation expenses
- ☐ Salary review
- ☐ Laptop/cell phone/PDA/company car
- ☐ Paid parking

Rejecting Job Applicants

Informing job applicants they did not get the job can be unpleasant—especially if the candidate was a final contender and may be expecting an offer. It's important to understand that you are not legally bound to tell applicants anything when you reject them. In fact, most legal experts advise employers to provide as little information as possible to rejected candidates.

Many employers today simply state that the candidate was not a "good fit" for the job. However, there are a few instances when you may want to provide applicants with a more detailed explanation of your decision. Specifically, you may feel it is necessary to give more feedback to a candidate who has been through several interviews or who applied for an executive or professional position. During the job interview process, it is a good idea to mention that there are many other applicants for the job. That way, an applicant may be less likely to think they've got the job—and cry foul when they don't get it.

It is also important to be tactful when informing applicants they did not get the position. This approach will help you maintain a professional image of your company. Word gets around fast if you're the kind of employer who dumps rejected job applicants, takes too long to inform them or doesn't inform them at all. It will also help you avoid getting sued. If a candidate is a minority, is a woman, is over 50 years old or has a disability, they could claim "discrimination" when rejected, rather than accepting they were not right for the job.

When should you inform a rejected applicant of your decision? If you have a lot of applicants to choose from, it's okay to contact rejected applicants as soon as you've eliminated them from the pool of possibilities. However, if you only have a few qualified candidates, it makes more sense to inform the rejected applicants only after the candidate you have chosen has accepted the job and started working and you feel like they are going to work out.

Q: Should I send a letter or call the applicant?

A: There's no one right answer. If you call, you may find yourself in an argument over why the rejected candidate wasn't chosen. By sending a letter, you can avoid confrontations.

Tips for rejecting applicants:

- **Do not tell the person you hired someone better qualified.** Say you hired someone who was more appropriate for the job.

- **Be honest.** Do not say the position is filled when it isn't—just to get someone off your back.

- **Avoid suggesting another position may be coming up** if you know in your heart the person would not be a viable candidate.

- **Do not be bullied into giving more information than you should.** Even if the rejected applicant threatens a lawsuit, be polite and end the conversation.

- **Do say:**

  — "Your qualifications are impressive, but unfortunately someone else's experience was more tailored to the unique requirements of this position."

  — "As you can imagine, we had many people apply for this one job. I will be happy to keep your application on file."

  — "You were not a good fit for this position."

Q: If a rejected job applicant calls me and demands to know why they weren't hired, what should I say?

A: You are under no obligation to explain why you picked one candidate over another. In fact, you're wise not to do so. At the most, simply say the candidate was not a good fit. And leave it at that—without going into any detail about education, experience or other factors.

Sample letter of rejection:

Dear (name),

Thank you very much for interviewing with me for the position of Direct Mail Specialist.

Although your background is impressive, we have offered the position to another applicant whose credentials and experience more closely meet our needs.

We will keep your application and résumé on file for one year. If a suitable opening occurs within that time, we will contact you.

Thank you for your interest in our company. I wish you the best of luck in your job search.

Sincerely,

John Doe, Manager, ABC Department

Worksheet: How would you respond if challenged by a rejected applicant?

If applicant asked the following questions, how would you respond?

- Can you give me feedback on why you didn't hire me? _____

_____

- Can I see my scores on the pre-employment test you gave me? _____

_____

- Can you tell me what my references said when you called?_____

_____

- Will you tell me what the other managers I met with thought about me? _____

_____

- Was my education the reason why you didn't hire me? _____

_____

Make sure you're prepared with a legally sound answer—and not caught off guard.

CHAPTER 5

Orienting, Training and Retaining Your Staff

After spending as much time as you do hiring good people, it only makes sense that you put as much—or more—time and effort into retaining them. Although you may feel there is nothing you can do to keep a good employee on your payroll, in reality there is a lot.

The people you hire stay on the job for a lot of different reasons. Of course, good money, health insurance and a 401(k) are important components in keeping people happy. But it has been proven time and again that these factors are not the most important. What employees want is to be recognized, feel valued, be given feedback regularly, be challenged—all things that may not cost you a dime. In this section, we'll look at how to make keeping good employees a top priority—starting the day your new hires walk in the door.

Bringing New Employees Onboard

Studies show many new hires question their decision to join their new employer by the end of the first day on the job. And as many as 60% of them quit within the first 10 days of starting. What a waste of your time and your company's money. Don't let this happen to you. Take the time and make the effort to bring new hires onboard in a way that makes them feel valued and welcomed and prepared to handle the challenges ahead. This will help them adjust to their jobs, get integrated into your work environment and develop a positive attitude and motivation from day one.

In HR circles, the latest approach to employee orientation is called "onboarding." It is a systematic, planned effort to make employee orientation fun, interesting, exciting, painless and simple. The idea is to make new hires feel valued, wanted, welcomed and excited—from day one. By doing so, you can inspire new employees to give their best and become of great value to your organization.

An employee's first day anxieties are fueled by having an employee handbook thrown at them … being forced to sit through boring company videos … being overwhelmed with facts and figures, names and titles … signing tons of paperwork and forms … finding they have no phone or computer or e-mail address. A planned onboarding experience can help you eliminate these worries. Even if your company has not formally adopted an onboarding approach to employee orientation, there are still many things managers can do to get employees up to speed faster and become contributors to your organization's goals.

Tips for creating a successful onboarding experience:

- Stay in touch with new hires after they accept their positions and before they actually start. You don't want them to have buyer's remorse and not show up.

- Post new employee information on your company intranet. This will answer many questions and get employees familiar with your company before arriving.

- Make sure employees are informed of your workplace rules and regulations, nuances and traditions. For example, if there is a dress code but it is relaxed on certain days, alert your employee so they don't come dressed inappropriately.

- Give employees information about company benefits and perks. Let them know exactly what they are eligible for and when.

- Post policies and procedures somewhere in writing. An on-line source that can easily be accessed and updated is ideal.

- Assign a mentor to the employee who can show them around, make introductions and answer questions.

- Prepare the employee's work area in advance. Make sure everything they may need to start their jobs—a computer, special equipment, instructions—is there.

- Be there to greet new hires the first morning and convey the message that they are important.

- Let co-workers know the employee is arriving so they can make a point to say hello.

- Give the employee the basic information they need to get started—the essentials of their job and how they are expected to handle them.

- Provide a list of contacts with names, titles, telephone numbers and e-mail addresses.

- Periodically ask the new hire how they're doing. Don't hesitate to modify the orientation you have planned in response to this feedback.

Worksheet: Orienting employees

Could your orientation process stand some improvement? Check whether the statements below are true or false:

True ___ False ___ Each new employee goes through a planned orientation program.

True ___ False ___ I make it a point to be there the first day to welcome my direct reports.

True ___ False ___ I do not cram everything into the first day. Orientation is a process that extends over several days.

True ___ False ___ A new hire is never left alone at lunch. If I am unable to take him or her out, I assign another appropriate person to.

True ___ False ___ I stay in close touch with employees after they accept the job and before they begin.

Were you able to answer "True" to all of the above? Hopefully, the answer is "yes."

Setting Up Personnel Files

Most managers have little interest in dealing with personnel paperwork. But taking the time to set up and maintain personnel files will pay off in a number of ways. First, you will be able to quickly access information about the employee should you need it. Your organization will expect a fast response. Also, at some point if you decide it is time for a poor performer to go, you'll be able to go to the file for documentation of the employee's past performance, any history of problems and specific discussions you've had together. The final and most important reason to keep good personnel files is this: Federal and state laws require you to keep certain records in certain situations. And if you are unexpectedly audited, you'll have no worries.

What should—and shouldn't—be in an employee's personnel file? There is no law requiring you to keep personnel records. However, once the job applicant accepts your offer, it's a good idea to start gathering the following information:

- Job application, résumé and job offer letter
- Any notes you've made when calling the applicant's references
- Signed acknowledgment the applicant has seen the employee handbook
- IRS Form W-4—determines how much to withhold from every paycheck for taxes
- Who to contact in case of emergency
- New hire reporting form—depending on your state—usually must be filed within 20 days after hiring someone
- Non-compete agreement—if applicable to the job
- Confidentiality agreement—if applicable to the job
- Benefit enrollment paperwork—showing if the employee wants health insurance, a 401(k) or other benefits your company offers
- Signed acknowledgment the employee has received company property—such as a laptop, cell phone or car
- Performance evaluations
- Any written documentation of performance problems—like memos or warnings
- Any recognition of excellent performance—such as awards or compliments
- Record of training completed
- Record of pay increases, promotions and bonuses
- Documents relating to the employee's departure, whether voluntary or involuntary

Do NOT include in the general personnel file the following—these records should be kept in separate files:

- Medical records—HIPAA requires employers and health care providers to keep medical records confidential, separate and apart from other business records.
- Any medical records related to a disabled employee
- I-9 form ensuring the employee is legally permitted to work in the United States
- Certain payroll records
- Records of your safety training efforts—this is required by OSHA and may be requested during an inspection
- Investigation records—they may contain embarrassing or extremely personal information that, if released, could lead to an invasion of privacy lawsuit
- Unnecessary comments about an employee's personal life, race, sex or religion—these could turn into evidence and come back to haunt you
- Health insurance application form
- Life insurance application form
- Request for medical leave of absence regardless of reason
- Personal accident reports
- Workers' compensation report of injury or illness
- OSHA injury and illness reports
- Physician records of examination, diagnostic records, laboratory test records
- Drug screening records
- Information related to investigations, such as disciplinary and sexual harassment
- Discrimination complaint investigation information
- Accusations of policy/legal violations
- Background investigation information
- Personal credit history
- Personal criminal conviction history
- Arrest records

Tip: In general, treat all medical information about all employees as confidential.

Maintaining employee records and managing highly confidential information is not a task to be taken lightly. Judges and lawmakers are closely focused on protecting the privacy rights of job applicants and employees. Maintain your employee's privacy by following these guidelines:

- Do not let just anyone see an employee's file. It should be accessed only by those who have a job-related need to know the information.

- All personnel files should be maintained in a secure setting under lock and key to ensure that access is limited.

- Do not allow employees to have custody of their own files. All files should be maintained in a central location.

- Information relating to an employee should be released only on a need-to-know basis or if a law requires the release of the information.

- Keep employees informed about what's being put into their files—especially in the case of negative information or disciplinary action. Employees need to know where they stand.

Q: Do my employees have the right to see their own files whenever they feel like it?

A: Most states say that they do have the right to confirm information in their file and identify information that needs to be corrected. So check your state laws on access to privacy records.

However, employers do have the right to control the time and location of employee examinations. Here are some guidelines for employers:

- You can limit the frequency of access to a certain number of times per year.

- You can request that employees ask in advance to see their files so that you have time to review the file.

- You can decide when and where the employee may examine the file—so it will not interfere with your schedule or the employee's.

- You can require the employee to view the file only in your presence or the presence of someone else you designate.

- You may also limit the information that the employee can see, depending on your state law.

Q: Is it okay to allow another manager to see my employee's personnel file?

A: Only managers who have a legitimate reason to see an employee's file should be allowed access. For example, a manager may be considering inviting your employee to be on a special team and may need to review their file to ensure the employee is qualified.

Worksheet: Personnel file review

Periodically, you should conduct a review of your employees' personnel files to ensure they are complete and accurate and do not contain unnecessary information. Place a checkmark by each item as you complete this review:

☐ Contains every written evaluation of the employee

☐ Contains promotions and commendations

☐ Shows every warning or other disciplinary action taken

☐ Indicates the removal of any written warnings or other disciplinary records that should have been removed after a certain period

☐ Shows the completion of any performance improvement plan, probationary or training period

☐ Contains a sign-off form showing the employee has seen the employee handbook if it has been updated since employment began

☐ Contains every contract or other agreement between me and the employee

☐ Does not contain I-9 forms or any medical information—these items are kept in separate files

Training Employees

Ideally, your new employees will already have all the skills they need to perform the job. But in the real world, many don't and need training to get up to speed. Training may be time-consuming and expensive. But it's important—you want well-qualified people who can do the jobs you hired them to do. Plus, the opportunity to continue to grow and develop through training and development is one of the most important factors in employee motivation.

TIP: Studies show the most successful employees are those who have been well-trained.

In addition, OSHA considers safety training the employer's obligation. OSHA has many rules about who is to be trained on what. You need to pay attention to OSHA's rules, especially when it comes to controlling hazards and using chemicals and certain equipment. Plus, many state laws require training on sexual harassment and other forms of harassment and discrimination.

There are many reasons why managers don't train their employees: They don't have time … they don't know how … they don't know what type of material to use—books, videos, pre-packaged training programs … they're not sure how to measure the value of the training their employees receive … they don't know how to make sure employees retain what they learn and apply it on the job.

But training is appropriate—and recommended—when:

- You uncover—in a performance appraisal or day-to-day coaching—a performance gap

- You are conducting an overall professional development program

- You are preparing an employee to assume a new role

- Knowledge about a particular topic is needed because of a change in your company or industry

- You're introducing a new technology or system

Unless you have unlimited funds, you need to determine your training needs and prioritize your efforts accordingly. Ask yourself: What will be the return on investment if I implement this training? For example, computer training can speed up productivity, customer service training can reduce the number of complaints you receive and communication training can sidestep many conflicts between employees.

Don't make the mistake of offering one-size-fits-all training and expecting it to work for every employee. People learn in many different ways. Give your employees options that suit their learning styles, for example:

- Seminars, workshops and classes
- Self-study manuals
- Video
- Computer-based
- On-the-job training
- Cross-training
- Field trips to other companies and organizations in your industry, field or city
- Adult education classes at local colleges and universities, community colleges or technical schools—including MBA programs
- Professional association workshops and conferences
- Business books purchased for employee use

Tips for training employees:

- Think of training as an investment in the future—not a cost.
- Evaluate which skills are most important to the success of your area and company and focus on those.
- Send a clear message that continual learning is vital. Encourage employees to keep their skills up to date and stay on top of their field and industry.
- Ask for upper management's support once you've identified mission-critical training topics.
- Create a basic training program, deliver it to a small group and then use their feedback to tweak it. Then roll it out.
- Get the best instructors and materials possible—from either inside or outside your company.
- Recognize and award employees who complete training.

- Continue to train and don't limit the training to new hires. Make it available to everyone.

- Measure your results. Establish your own benchmark for success and see if you're getting an appropriate return on investment. Upper management will want proof before giving you funding in the future.

- If possible, provide tuition assistance.

Worksheet: Making training work

You are not alone if training you have offered in the past did not pay off. Changing employee behavior is hard. You can, however, do many things in advance of training to ensure it sticks. Circle which of the steps below you are following:

- I complete a needs analysis to determine if there is a true need for training.

- I let my employees know why the new skills are important and how the training we are offering is linked to their job.

- I describe how the training will improve the employee's ability to contribute to the achievement of our corporate goals.

- I recognize employees who complete training and reward them with a certificate or by listing their name in our company newsletter.

- I reinforce that training is the employee's responsibility and I expect active participation and an effort to apply in the workplace skills learned.

- I make sure the training directly relates to the skills I want the employee to master.

- I make sure the training has clearly stated and measurable objectives and outcomes that transfer back to the job—so the employee will know how to apply the information learned in the real world.

Managing Your Employees' Career Development

If you're thinking that managing the career development of your employees is not your job, think again. One of a manager's key responsibilities is the development of staff. That includes encouraging growth by helping employees reach their personal goals.

Career development refers to a broad category of activities that may include policies and practices designed to improve the employee's growth and advancement over the course of their career. It is ongoing, dynamic and focused on two areas:

1. Mastering skills and knowledge necessary to perform the job

2. Mastering skills and knowledge that go beyond the scope of the job but still directly improve performance

Why bother to support career development?

- You can help employees create realistic career development goals based on industry trends and your company's needs.

- You can provide opportunities for promotions and/or lateral moves.

- You can build employee self-confidence by giving them responsibility for managing their own careers.

- You can increase employee motivation and productivity.

- You will be in a better position to attract and keep top employees when you show your support for their career development.

Employees don't want to feel stuck in their jobs with no advancement opportunities or challenges to look forward to. It's important you be responsible—and accountable—for their career development. This may involve assessing and providing feedback on their skills and interests, providing training and development activities that match their career objectives and job needs and annually having career discussions with employees.

Usually, the key components of career development are:

- Career planning
- Education and training
- Promotion opportunities

Tips for supporting employee career development:

- Set aside uninterrupted time to discuss career development.
- Assist employees in setting realistic career goals based on the needs in your department and company.
- Create formal opportunities for skill development, such as job rotation, cross-training, mentoring and internships.
- Agree to release time when it's necessary for staff development.
- Let employees know about career opportunities within your organization.
- Be a role model—take part in career and professional development opportunities yourself.
- Engage employees in two-way dialogue about their future careers.
- Don't get angry when employees apply for other positions—see this as a sign of a healthy and growing workforce.
- Show them how to identify their skills, interests and values.
- Conduct performance appraisals that carefully point out strengths as well as areas the employee can work on.
- Create an individual development plan for each employee and use it as a springboard for discussions.
- Provide opportunities for employees to gain experience, exposure and visibility in your organization.

Worksheet: Expanding an employee's job responsibilities

One of the best ways to support career development is by expanding an employee's job responsibilities. Take this quiz to look at possible ways you can do a better job of this. Use the following rating:

A = Always

B = Most of the time

C = Occasionally

D = Really need to work on this

_____ I see an employee's request to take on more responsibilities as the sign of a healthy workplace.

_____ I enable employees to attend and participate in important meetings with or without me.

_____ I include employees on specific mailing lists, so they receive company briefings and notices that have previously been restricted.

_____ I encourage employees to set goals, establish priorities and create measurements.

_____ I give them new, more challenging responsibilities.

_____ I re-assign to someone else those responsibilities that have become routine and unchallenging for employees.

_____ I give employees the authority to manage their time and schedules and to make decisions.

_____ I invite employees to get involved in bigger-picture planning in my department or in company-wide initiatives.

_____ I give employees supervisory or team leadership responsibilities.

_____ As the boss, I spend one-on-one time with employees.

_____ I allow employees to cross-train in other roles, areas and responsibilities.

Do you see areas where you can expand your employees' jobs even more?

Retaining Employees

Have you noticed how difficult it is to find good people to fill your job openings? Have you also noticed how painful it is when the good people you do hire leave? Every time a great employee leaves, you have to shell out the cost of rehiring and retraining a replacement—a cost that studies have shown could range from 70 – 200% of that person's annual salary. And with each employee who leaves, you also lose that employee's institutional memory, another great asset for your company.

You need to make keeping good employees a top priority. But what does it take to retain employees? Today's employees are looking for more than good pay. They want a friendly work environment where they feel valued, they have some decision-making authority, they feel part of the team—and they feel they are making a real contribution to your organization's vision and goals.

You can address these issues proactively—before they become problems—by following a few suggestions:

- **Reward high performance in whatever ways you can**. A cash bonus is nice, but it's not the only way to reward employees. And it's easy for employees to start expecting money every time they perform. A better reward may be non-monetary—like giving away tickets to an event, giving time off, sending the employee to a professional conference or paying for special training.

- **Create traditions employees enjoy and look forward to**—like a dress-up day for Halloween, summer picnic, spring retreat. Or perhaps bring in pizza at the end of a hard week.

- **Think diversity when hiring employees.** Hiring employees who are all basically the same is boring. Having a workforce of people of different genders and race, from different parts of the country and world and from different socio-economic backgrounds, makes work a lot more interesting.

- **Be sensitive** to employees' personal lives and the changes they go through. The birth of a baby, the death of a parent, unexpected health issues, the need to take care of an ailing family member—these situations are part of life and shouldn't be ignored. By recognizing these changes, you can show employees you care and you can perhaps help them find solutions—so when they are at work they can give 100% to their jobs.

- **Be a great boss.** Think back to that great boss you had. You'd do anything for him or her, wouldn't you? Your employees will follow you wherever you lead if you show you're a good leader.

- **Have how's-it-going talks with employees.** You know who your best employees are. You don't want to lose them, do you? Make a point of telling them how much you appreciate the job they are doing. Encourage them to think about taking on more responsibility and challenge and playing a bigger part in the success of your company. By keeping in close touch with their needs, you can hopefully avoid the day when your best employee comes in and unexpectedly announces "I quit."

- **Give employees the freedom to innovate.** If you have someone who is eager to develop and implement their own ideas in your company, don't squelch their passion. Encourage their innovation. Give them time to work on special projects. Make sure they have the resources they need to bring their ideas to fruition.

- **Don't expect employees to be on call 24/7.** They have personal lives, families and obligations beyond your company. Today's generation in particular is not willing to give their whole life to "The Company." Provide flextime and allow employees to work at home once in a while. Be sensitive to how many hours employees are working and how their home lives may become strained. Sometimes the job calls for long hours. But make this the exception, not the standard.

- **Share your vision.** Employees do not do well working in a vacuum. They need to know where you and the company are headed—especially in times of growth or change, like during mergers and acquisitions. By spending time with employees to remind them why you all are there, you can calm any fears and build the sense that "we're all in this together."

- **Have fun.** It's so easy to get overly involved in the day-to-day drudgery of work and deadlines that we forget completely about having a little fun. Take a moment every once in a while to laugh, let your hair down, tell a joke and enjoy. It's a great way to get to know employees and reduce stress at the same time.

- **Celebrate employees' start date anniversaries**, birthdays, promotions, new babies and other special events. Thank employees and teams when they do a good job. You can send them a handwritten note, recognize them in a public meeting or feature them in your company newsletter. The important thing is the recognition—individuals as well as teams thrive on it.

CHAPTER 6

Maintaining High Performance

To succeed as a manager and to ensure your employees succeed, you need to manage their performance—and *not* just once a year with an annual performance review. You need to manage performance day by day through regular communication, feedback, goal setting, rewards, diagnosing performance problems and coaching. In other words, you need a performance management system. Even if your company does not have a formal performance management system in place, you can still reap the benefits—employees who are motivated to achieve the best possible performance.

Managing Employee Performance

Performance management boils down to creating an environment that builds employee commitment and performance. It's not something you do once a year. It's an ongoing process that involves a cycle of planning what needs to be done, checking in with employees to ensure it is being done and assessing how well it was done.

Your role in performance management includes these key activities:

- **Clearly defining employee job duties and your expectations.** Employees rise to the occasion when they know exactly what they are supposed to do and why. Your job, as the boss, is to define their specific job responsibilities and communicate them clearly so they know the what, why and when of their positions. You need to set daily, monthly and yearly goals that are aligned with your company's objectives … develop standards of performance that will tell you if the employee has succeeded … drive home how the employee's contributions really do make a difference to the success of your company … and define success in your department and company and what employees need to know and do to achieve it.

- **Communicating with employees frequently and constructively.** You can't give employees their goals and then not check up on their progress until the end of the year. You need to observe and monitor their performance day by day, give them regular feedback on what they're doing right and wrong and keep a two-way flow of communication going. You have an array of formal and informal tools to draw from—such as informal talks, quarterly discussions, once-a-year reviews—to help you feel confident employees have the information they need to do their job. And to be sure you can catch small problems before they grow into big ones. Group status meetings are important as are status reports. But don't underestimate the power of quick, two-minute talks with employees, held throughout the day.

- **Rewarding employees for the right behaviors.** Motivating employees must be one of your top priorities. One of the best ways to keep employees motivated and focused on your goals and the bottom line is through rewards. Now you don't have to give employees big sums of money to empower them and keep their engines going. You can give them time off, recognize them in a group meeting, even say thank you once in a while. You'll be surprised how far these small actions go.

- **Diagnosing and addressing the real causes of performance failure.** Sooner—rather than later—employees will fail to meet your expectations. That's the nature of the management game. They'll habitually be late for work or not show up at all. They'll procrastinate, complain and cause conflicts. That's when you need to figure out the real causes underlying these performance problems so they can be eliminated as swiftly as possible. Could your work system be at fault, making it virtually impossible for an employee to succeed—because of too much red tape or poor processes and procedures? You need to find out the root causes. And that calls for a heart-to-heart meeting to which you bring the facts—not your emotions.

Let's probe deeper into this difficult area ...

Identifying the Causes of Poor Performance

Nonperformance issues are a major managerial headache. And do they ever cost—organizations spend millions of dollars dealing with less-than-satisfactory quality, poor productivity and turnover. In fact, the cost is so high you simply cannot overlook a problem or minimize it.

Why do employees miss deadlines, show up late, make mistakes and fail to perform to the standards you've set? It's never easy to uncover the real reason. But you can't solve the problem if you don't know what's causing it. The solution will depend on what the problem is, so diagnosis is important. The most important thing is to get started.

The truth is, poor performance can result from even a single problem or barrier that is allowed to fester. And too often the manager works on the wrong cause and so performance never improves.

Here are some of the most common reasons for performance failure:

- Failure to understand what it is they're supposed to do
- Uncertainty about how to perform their duties
- Lack of skills
- No recognition
- Barriers in the work process
- Standards are set too high
- No motivation

- Failure to see why their job is important

- Personal problems

- Supervisor has low expectations

- Lack of commitment

- Lack of proper tools, equipment or supplies

TIP: It helps to think of diagnosing performance problems as a problem-solving process—rather than a punishing process. You don't want to put employees on the defensive.

Tips for uncovering the reasons why an employee is failing:

- Ask if your work processes or systems could be causing the person to fail. Is there a slowdown somewhere? Are the goals impossible to meet? Could another department be getting in the way?

- Check the employee's job description. Is it aligned with your company's objectives? Are there any discrepancies? How could you bring them back into line?

- Clearly communicate your expectations. Does the employee understand the work that is to be accomplished? The standards you use to evaluate their success?

- Give the employee feedback. Have you honestly told the employee your concerns? Have you been constructive—not destructive—in your comments?

- Coach the employee. Have you provided the tools and resources the employee needs to succeed? Are you staying in touch constantly and regularly to improve performance before it's too late?

- Evaluate the employee's strengths and weaknesses. Have you explained how you came to the conclusions you did—based on checklists, peer evaluations or other tools—so the employee is able to correct the problem?

- Provide support in their career development. Does the employee know you are willing to assist in skill development and professional growth?

Worksheet: Diagnosing performance problems

1. Pick a performance problem you have been trying to change but with no luck.

   Identify the employee involved.

   Name: _____

   Briefly describe the problem: _____

   _____

2. Ask yourself:

   • Does the employee know what is expected?   Yes   No

   • Does the employee have the right skills?   Yes   No

   • Does the employee have the necessary tools and resources?   Yes   No

   • Could a personal problem be contributing to the problem?   Yes   No

3. If you can't answer these questions, who can?

   ____The employee   ____Someone else

4. Based on your answers to these questions, what is your plan of action?

   _____

   _____

   _____

   _____

   _____

   _____

Confronting Behavior Problems

Have you noticed how much time and energy you spend dealing with problem employees—employees who:

- Don't follow your directions

- Spend too much time on the phone

- Fail to follow procedures

- Abuse the Internet

- Arrive late, leave early and take "a few minutes" extra at lunch

- Bully other employees and try to control people through fear

- Start and feed rumors and personally attack others

- Are opinionated, bull-headed and rude

- Are pessimistic and try to bring others down with them

- Do the least amount of work possible to just get by

- Bring all their personal problems to work and spend hours cornering co-workers with their day-to-day dramas

- Need constant reassurance from others that they are doing a good job

- Challenge your authority and question your decisions

It's one of the most challenging and draining parts of a manager's job. Difficult employees will test your limits and threaten productivity and—in the worst cases—the negative effects of their unacceptable behavior can infect your entire team.

When an employee's behavior is unacceptable, don't wait, simply hoping it will get better. It probably won't. You must address the issue immediately. Otherwise, the other people working for you may start to wonder why you're not doing anything about it—and see you as weak. Failure to confront the person can cause legal trouble too. Often, it is the employee with frequent conflicts with management who ends up filing a lawsuit later.

You can't dive unprepared into discussions with employees about sensitive behavior issues. You have to be strategic about it. And you need to handle each employee fairly, legally and with professionalism—so you don't damage morale, yet still get lasting results.

Level 1—Informal discussion: Unless the behavior problem is serious—like an employee who threatens another with violence—you want to address the behavior at the lowest level. This may be as simple as taking employees aside and reminding them of the rules—assuming an employee has not read or understood them. Draw to their attention the fact that they signed a form saying they were given the employee handbook. Explain that you will give it a reasonable amount of time and then get back with the employee to review how things are going. If training or coaching is needed, be sure to arrange it. Be low-key and friendly in this discussion.

Level 2—Formal counseling session: If the chat does no good and the behavior continues, it's time to schedule a more formal—but still friendly—counseling session between you and the employee. Meet in the employee's office—not yours. You want to avoid making employees feel like you're bossing them around. Calling an employee into your office can put them on the defensive. Confront the problem head on. Clear the air and acknowledge that there is an issue. Say: "When I ask you to do (___), I expect you to do it."

Make sure the employee understands. Require the employee to confirm what you just said and what is expected. Practice what you're going to say. Don't wing it. If you have a mental script you'll be less likely to get off track. Follow-up with an e-mail or memo. Summarize what you discussed and the timetable for changes to be made.

Tips for confronting problem behavior:

- Be alert to early warning signs and address them before a bigger problem occurs.

- Be willing to look deeper than the anger, poor attitude, tardiness or other problem behavior. Try to find the root cause.

- Honestly ask yourself if you are contributing to the problem—for example, maybe your management style is harsh or your closed door policy discourages employees from discussing problems with you.

- Trust your intuition. If an employee seems to be avoiding you or is reluctant to talk to you, there may be something else going on.

- Gather all the facts before confronting the employee. Talk to others and get their views of the situation.

- Treat employees with respect. Do not berate, punish or degrade them.

- Get agreement between you and the employee about the solution and the steps needed to be taken to resolve the problem.

Q: I suspect two employees are involved in a romance. What should I as the manager do?

A: If the romance presents a serious threat to your work group or morale or if it lowers productivity, then some form of intervention is required. You need to know when disciplinary action is needed—and what's appropriate—if the romance derails and the behavior of the dating couple disrupts the workplace. If the romance becomes sexual harassment, you not only need to know but you also need to take immediate action.

Worksheet: Could you be part of the problem?

It's easy for managers to fall into the trap of denying there is a problem—or putting off addressing it. Circle whether you agree or disagree with each of the following statements to become more aware of how you view yourself in this area.

Agree/Disagree

A   D   I tend to deny the seriousness of the problem by rationalizing or justifying it.

A   D   I hope the poor behavior will improve on its own.

A   D   I spend too much time worrying about the behavior and the employee.

A   D   I feel sorry for employees who complain about personal problems and how they keep them from doing their jobs.

A   D   Sometimes I take over the duties of an employee who isn't doing the job.

A   D   Sometimes I try to avoid the problem employee.

A   D   My expectations for the problem employee have lowered over time.

A   D   I am afraid to confront some employees because I don't want them to hate me.

A   D   Sometimes I make excuses for a problem employee.

If you answered "Agree" to any of these statements, you may be part of the problem. You need to stop enabling and start confronting problem employees.

Conducting Annual Performance Appraisals

Performance appraisals are met with dread by employees and managers alike. Managers feel uncomfortable confronting employees and discussing sensitive issues. Employees feel like the boss focuses only on what's wrong and that they're being unfairly scrutinized and punished.

But both are missing the point. If approached and done correctly—and with the right attitude—performance appraisals are a great way to open the lines of communication, measure employee success and set future goals. They can both ensure that the employee's needs are being met and your organization's goals are being achieved and can become a meeting everyone looks forward to.

Before you conduct a performance appraisal, be sure you know what you can and can't say. Even one slip of the tongue can come back to haunt you and result in charges of discrimination—and even lawsuits.

Here are some common pitfall areas to avoid:

- Do not make comments based on stereotypes—like gender—rather than on fact. For example, do not rate a male higher than a female based solely on gender.

- Do not assume an employee is a good performer simply because the employee has been with your company 30 years.

- Do not allow emotions and personal feelings to get in the way. For example, don't give an employee a good review because you car pool with them.

- Do not fear confrontations so much that you rate poorly performing employees higher than you should.

- Do not fail to document what's said. Documentation may be your only defense should you be called into court.

Tips for conducting effective performance appraisals:

- Schedule the first review for six months after the employee joins your department or organization. Schedule the next one for six months later. Then you can adhere to the traditional once a year schedule.

- Read the notes you've been making throughout the year about the employee's performance. If you haven't been taking notes, start this important practice immediately.

- Initiate the meeting. Tell the employee when the meeting is and what the process involves. Give them a copy of the appraisal form in advance so they can read it and think about the past year and their performance.

- Ask the employee if their job description needs to be updated because of changes in duties. Get their recommendations for how to update it. Be sure they have a job description in advance so they can think about it.

- Don't make any comments related to race, sex, religion, national origin, handicap or veteran status.

- Go over both positive and negative events, interactions and attitudes.

- Record employee accomplishments, strengths, weaknesses and obstacles and suggest how the employee can improve performance through training and development.

- Document your input.

- Be specific and concrete. Instead of saying "you need to do better in this area," you need to define the exact behavior you expect, in what areas, with whom and how. For example: "I expect you to increase the number of accounts you open by 10% by December 31."

- Let the employee speak first. Avoid sounding defensive. End on a positive note.

- Do not surprise the employee with performance issues you haven't previously discussed. Surprises make it look like you're not doing your job monitoring performance nor being fair.

- Be sure to rate the employee's performance for the entire year—rather than let a recent good or bad incident color your opinion.

- Don't list all the things the employee is doing wrong while skimming over the good things. Be fair and objective.

- Don't guess why an employee did or didn't act in a certain way. Get the facts.

- Be prepared to back up your comments with specific examples.

- End the session with agreement between you and the employee on measurable and achievable goals for the next year.

Q: I am worried abut bringing up a difficult issue in an upcoming performance evaluation meeting. This employee does not like to be told what to do—especially by authority figures.

A: Temper your criticisms by enlisting the person's input and advice. For example, if mistakes are the problem, first try to discover why the mistakes are occurring. Then ask the employee to come up with a solution that will work. When people feel like they own a problem, they are more likely to be less defensive.

Q: I will be expected to evaluate an employee I hardly know. How should I approach the session?

A: If you can, find someone who is familiar with the employee and suggest she or he do the review. Or at least get this person's input. If there's no way out, review the information you do have about the employee—like a job description, last year's review documentation, memos and status reports. Look at the employee's accomplishments and goals. Together, develop a plan for the upcoming year.

Tip: The best appraisal begins long before the annual meeting. By being a presence in your employee's life and giving regular feedback, you can approach the annual review with no stress—and no surprises.

Motivating and Rewarding Employees

How much could you accomplish if all your employees arrived highly motivated, committed and energized—every day? Motivated employees are a huge asset to the organization. They show initiative, have energy, share ideas and eagerly take on more challenges and responsibilities. But not every employee is motivated. Inevitably, you will have less-than-enthusiastic workers who come in late, watch the clock, cut corners and slack off until quitting time.

Dealing with the unmotivated employee is incredibly frustrating and time-consuming. And their lackluster performance takes a toll on productivity and morale. That's why motivation issues cannot go unaddressed.

Disappointed in an employee's performance? Could lack of motivation be the problem? The answer may be yes if these signs are evident:

- **Changes in attitude.** Did the employee used to be cheerful and positive, but now seems withdrawn, detached or moody?

- **Tardiness.** Has a normally prompt and reliable employee started to come in late or leave early?

- **Inability to handle stress.** Does the employee have a good track record for completing projects and assignments, but now seems stressed, short-tempered and hard to get along with?

- **Change in lunch and coffee breaks.** Does the employee take more time than usual—or not take them at all?

- **Problems getting along with people.** Was the employee a team player before, but now has conflicts and disagreements with people?

- **More mistakes.** Have you noticed more errors being made—like misspelled words, accounting or equipment set-up problems?

- **Drop in productivity.** Is the employee taking longer to complete assignments? Is the quality of those projects less than before?

If you do suspect there is a motivation problem, the next question is: How can I motivate the employee? That's a tough question—and there's no simple, one-size-fits-all approach, formula or worksheet. There are two general approaches to motivation. You can motivate on the spot by intimidating employees or striking fear into their hearts. They'll do what you need to have done. But this approach can be hurtful and harmful and produce only short-term results. A better way to motivate is through constructive approaches—and by creating an environment where people want to do their best.

What DECREASES motivation:

- Work that is not challenging

- No opportunity for advancement

- Little or no recognition

- Isolation from the team

- Being left out of the loop—poor communication

- Unclear goals and expectations
- Creativity and ideas discouraged
- Being threatened for making mistakes

What FUELS motivation:

- Showing employees respect
- Challenging work
- Meaningful work
- Frequent feedback
- Clear expectations
- Any kind of recognition

While employees are ultimately responsible for motivating themselves, managers do have some responsibility for setting up an environment where they can motivate themselves. Here are some things you can do:

- **Ask employees what motivates them.** Each employee is an individual. Different employees are motivated by different things. One person may want more money, more recognition or an opportunity to attend a conference or take a course. Another employee may get excited about a simple thank you or an unexpected compliment.

- **Treat motivation as a process, not a single task.** It's something that requires your ongoing effort and may require you to re-think what you're doing as your organization and your people change.

- **Reward employees for their performance**—not their personalities. Recognize those behaviors that move your organization toward its goals.

- **Recognize behavior on the spot.** Praise employees for exceeding a goal. Applaud them for their teamwork. This will make a dramatic point that this is the behavior you want to see more of.

Can you afford to spend a little? Try these low-cost motivators:

- Give a day off with pay.
- Schedule off-site training.
- Sponsor a retreat off-site.
- Give away tickets to a sporting event.
- Give someone a better office location.
- Buy bagels for your entire staff.
- Pay for a weekend at a bed and breakfast inn or nice hotel.
- Send a personalized card to employees who've experienced a death or illness in the family.
- Have lunch catered by a favorite restaurant.
- Provide free soft drinks and other refreshments in the lunch room.
- Provide free popcorn one afternoon.
- Sponsor a picnic held on company time.
- Give employees a free pass or membership to a health club.

No budget? Try these no-cost motivators:

- Offer flextime. (Workers love this reward but managers often do not even consider it.)
- Give the person more authority.
- Send a personal, handwritten thank-you note.
- Catch someone doing a good job and compliment them on the spot.
- Let people choose the color of a new chair or a piece of artwork.
- Schedule a food day when all staff are invited to bring a dish.
- Praise employees in public—at a company meeting, for example.
- Make up a fun award and give it to someone each month.
- Allow a good employee to work from home one day a week.
- Schedule a casual Friday.
- Ask employees what pet project they'd like to do and then make it happen.

Q: Won't money always motivate people?

A: It may motivate some employees, but not all. Each person is different, which is why you must find out what motivates them, person by person. How do you do this? By observing them, listening to them—and, yes, by asking them!

Worksheet: What motivates your employees?

Identify a specific employee. Make a list of 3 – 5 things that you think motivates that person. Next ask the employee to fill out the list for themselves. Compare the answers. What did you learn?

Employee Name: _____

My list of what I think motivates this employee:

1. _____
2. _____
3. _____
4. _____
5. _____

The employee's list of things that are motivating:

1. _____
2. _____
3. _____
4. _____
5. _____

Surprised by the differences? Good thing you asked! Repeat this exercise for each of your employees.

CHAPTER 7

Disciplining and Firing

In today's workplace, discipline and termination should not be taken lightly. Both actions must be handled with care and skill. Every meeting must be choreographed in advance so nothing is left to chance. Every employee must be treated with dignity—if they aren't, the chances of that disgruntled person filing a wrongful discharge lawsuit increase. This section explains how to discipline problem employees—and fire them, if necessary—so your company doesn't suffer.

Taking Formal Disciplinary Action

Terminating an employee can cause more problems than you want in the long run. If you think you can salvage a problem employee, by all means try. It's better than going through the firing process—unless, of course, the person's behavior gives clear grounds for dismissal, as in the case of theft or violence.

If you've tried counseling the problem employee but have gotten no results or results that are not acceptable, it's time to begin progressive discipline—a series of increasingly formal efforts designed to help the employee overcome the problem and get back on track. Virtually all employers practice progressive discipline, whether they know it or not and whether it is formal or informal.

The goal of progressive discipline is not to punish or get rid of poor performers, but to get an employee's attention, help them understand a problem exists and show them they have the opportunity to improve. Ideally, progressive discipline results in improved performance. However, if it doesn't, the process will allow you to fairly and legally terminate any employee who is unwilling or unable to improve.

Adopting a program of progressive discipline will protect you in the long run. State your procedures in an employee handbook. List examples of behavior that can lead to discipline or firing, but make it clear that other behaviors may also lead to the same outcome.

Some offenses that may warrant disciplinary action are:

- **Insubordination.** Employee refuses to do what a supervisor instructs or orders (unless the instruction is illegal or unsafe).

- **Assault.** A verbal attack or the threat of physical violence

- **Battery.** An intentional act which results in physical contact

- **Abusive language.** Written or oral use of profane or obscene language

- **Showing disrespect.** Lack of consideration for another person

- **Absenteeism.** Employee frequently misses work

- **Imprisonment.** An employee is incarcerated or imprisoned and unable to work

- **Tardiness.** Employee arrives late to his or her work station

- **Leaving early.** Employee leaves for break, lunch or home before designated time

- **Misconduct.** Employee's behavior violates a company or departmental rule or policy

- **Dishonesty.** Behavior is clearly deceitful or untruthful

- **Inappropriate dress and grooming.** Employee does not meet established standards

- **Fighting.** Employee gets involved in an altercation

- **Horseplay.** Employee gets involved in "play" which could cause personal injury or property damage

- **Substance abuse.** Employee is under the influence of alcohol or controlled substances at work

- **Off-duty misconduct.** Employee's behavior while off duty harms the company's reputation or products

- **Moonlighting.** Employee's outside employment negatively affects the employee's job

- **Sleeping on the job.** Employee spends paid time in an unproductive manner

- **Unsatisfactory performance.** Employee is incompetent, unable to do the job, careless or negligent or has disregard for company property and rules

- **Sexual harassment.** An employee's unwelcome sexual advances or requests for sexual favors or other verbal or physical conduct of a sexual nature

Is progressive discipline appropriate? Think through the answers to these questions to make a determination:

- Does the problem disrupt productivity and workflow?

- Has it caused any damage to products or equipment?

- Does it create a safety hazard?

- Has or could an employee, customer or someone else suffer bodily injury as a result of the behavior?

- Is the behavior considered acceptable in terms of professional norms?

- Is the behavior in violation of a federal or state law?

- Has the behavior resulted in a waste of time, money or other organizational resources?

- Has the behavior affected the morale of other employees?

- How easily can the behavior be corrected?

- Could the behavior be a symptom of other, more serious problems?

- Has the behavior damaged your company's professional image?

- Has the behavior undermined your authority?

Although progressive discipline is used almost universally in companies, the manner in which it is implemented varies greatly. Typically, these are the general steps in a progressive discipline system:

- **Verbal reprimand.** Be specific about your concern and about what you expect to see as improvement. For example, "Joe, you have made the same proofing mistake three times in two days. All proofreaders are expected to turn in error-free work. I'll be closely monitoring your work in the future. If one more mistake occurs, I'll have to move on to the next disciplinary step."

- **Written warning.** This should contain a statement about the employee's history of performance, a statement about the current situation including the details of the most recent incident and a statement about the future, including your expectations and the consequences if the behavior does not change. Address the written warning to the employee and put it in his or her file. This step may be repeated with stronger consequence statements—for example: "This is a final warning. If (name) fails to correct the behavior, termination will result." The written warning should be direct and clear to the point. It should describe the correction steps you expect to see from the employee.

- **Suspension without pay.** Again, discuss the issue with the employee. The written record of suspension is prepared after this discussion. It specifies the start and end dates, stresses that this is a final warning, states the reason for the suspension, and is given to the employee.

- **Termination of the employee.** This is the last—and most serious—step in the progressive discipline process.

Tips for successful progressive discipline:

- First, thoroughly investigate the situation. Get the employee's explanation and any other supporting information.

- Document every step of the process. Should you end up in court, your documentation will be your defense.

- It's okay to repeat a step if time has passed and the problem has re-occurred.

- You don't have to be rigid about following the steps in the process. Some behavior—like physical assault or theft—may require you to take quick and severe action. Other behavior—like tardiness or excessive mistakes—may require all steps be followed.

- Sit down behind closed doors with the employee. Begin by describing in detail the behavior you have observed and why it concerns you.

- Don't point fingers and don't place blame.

- Ask for any reasons the employee can give for the behavior.

- Use reflective listening to hear the whole story.

- Tel the employee—in no uncertain terms—that the behavior must change immediately.

- Ask for the employee's input on how to solve the problem.

- Discuss each idea the employee offers.

- Together agree on a plan of action and what the expected results are.

- Leave the employee's self-esteem in tact. Reinforce how valuable the employee is to the team. Let the employee know you are confident he or she can change.

- Document the discussion.

- Close by setting a follow-up date when you will evaluate the employee's progress.

> **Q:** I just fired an employee who flagrantly disregarded her job responsibilities. Do I need to worry about legal backlash?
>
> **A:** You can't stop an employee from filing a lawsuit. But, if you followed due process by implementing all the steps of progressive discipline, you should be in a better position to prove you told the employee what was expected and the consequences of failing to meet those expectations.

Terminating Employees

There is nothing pleasant about terminating employees. Nevertheless, it is your job as a manager to get rid of employees who won't or can't do the job. That's why you must understand how to do it sensitively, with dignity and—above all—legally. First, you have to understand the concept of at-will employment.

At-will employment

The basic idea underlying at-will employment is this: An employee is hired at-will and employment can be terminated by either the employee or employer at any time and for any reason not prohibited by law, with or without prior cause or notice. Many managers mistakenly think this frees them from any obligation or liability. But this is hardly true. Employers may forfeit this right by statements or conduct that give employees assurances of job security or lead them to believe that they may be terminated only for cause. Such actions may expose an employer to wrongful termination or breach of contract claims.

That's why you must—during the hiring process and after it—let employees know they are at-will employees. That way you can rely on that statement as proof that you reserve the right to fire employees for any reason.

Many organizations protect their right to fire at will by requiring applicants and new employees to sign a written statement agreeing that they are employed at will. Such a statement hopefully appears on your employment application, in employment contracts and offer letters and in your employee handbook.

Wrongful discharge

While—unless an employee is under contract—you're free to fire the person at any time, for any reason or for no reason at all—an employee still can claim wrongful discharge and file a lawsuit against you. Employees can claim:

- The firing violated anti-discrimination laws. Federal and state statutes prohibit firings based on an employee's race, color, religion, sex, national origin, age or disability.

- The firing violated an implied contract with the employer. If you make a promise of job security when hiring an employee, many courts will take the employee's side.

- The firing violated public policy. You can't fire an employee in retaliation for whistle-blowing, refusing to participate in an illegal act or enforcing a legal right such as filing a workers' compensation claim.

Q: What if an employee I want to hire refuses to sign at at-will employment agreement?

A: Employees don't have to sign an at-will agreement. But most courts have supported employers' rights to fire or refuse to hire employees who won't sign it.

Q: I have a small company and can't afford to keep hiring "mistakes." How can I make sure I am able to legally fire employees I hire if they don't do the job or just don't work out, or if my business changes and I don't need them any longer?

A: First, make it clear in the hiring process you are an "at-will employer" and that at any time you can terminate the employee. Require the employee to sign an offer letter indicating he or she understands and agrees to this fact. For extra security, make sure there is an at-will statement in your employee handbook.

You can fire an employee who:

- Isn't able to perform the job and you have given him or her plenty of time and opportunity to succeed

- Violates a company policy that is clear, legal, established and distributed to employees

- Arrives late repeatedly or is absent frequently and so is unable to perform the job

- Is physically violent or threatens to be (This is grounds for immediate termination.)

- Comes to work under the influence of drugs or alcohol

- Commits an illegal act, such as theft or embezzlement

- Lies about information on their employment application or résumé

You cannot legally fire an employee on these grounds:

- Race, gender, national origin, disability, religion or age (if the person is over 40)

- For complaining about discrimination or harassment, filing a lawsuit or a charge or testifying in behalf of a co-worker who was discriminated against or harassed

- Refusing to take a lie detector test

- Lack of citizenship

- Whistle-blowing—complaining about illegal or unethical conduct in the workplace
- Refusal to commit an illegal act—like falsifying tax returns
- Exercising their right to vote
- Exercising their right to file a worker's compensation claim

Q: I am preparing to fire an employee who will probably fiercely argue my decision. What should I do?

A: Do not get into an argument with an employee you have terminated. Let the employee vent. But do not argue back—it could only hurt you later.

Worksheet: Making the decision to terminate

You've made the decision to fire an employee. But is it based on legally sound reasons? Answer the questions below to make sure.

Yes _____ No _____ The reason for firing is business-related and legitimate.

Yes _____ No _____ I have taken the time to investigate the situation.

Yes _____ No _____ I have documentation of the problem.

Yes _____ No _____ I have followed company policy.

Yes _____ No _____ My company has fired other people for similar reasons.

Yes _____ No _____ My decision to fire can be defended in court.

Yes _____ No _____ I have enlisted a second opinion to ensure the decision is fair and impartial.

Conducting the Termination Meeting

Now you're ready to conduct the termination meeting—assuming that you have followed all the steps of progressive discipline and the employee's behavior has not changed. Do not give the employee more than a few minutes' notice before the meeting. You will cause unnecessary stress and this could cause the employee to become angry or volatile. In addition to you and the employee, include someone from HR or another manager. The tone you set in the termination meeting is important. If the atmosphere is tense, highly emotional or negative, the employee may become more resentful and more likely to sue you later. Be courteous and treat the employee with respect.

Before the meeting:

- **Practice what you're going to say.** Think about what questions might come up and how you will answer them.

- **Plan to conduct the session in the morning if possible.** The employee will then have time to clean out their desk and depart and you won't be forced to be there alone after hours with him or her.

- **Never fire employees on a Friday.** The best day to fire them is early in the week, to give them sufficient time during the work week to seek other employment opportunities.

- **Don't fire on the spur of the moment.** You'll probably be angry—and the employee will likely respond in the same way.

- **Control the location of the termination meeting.** Ideally, fire employees in their own work area so that when you are finished you can walk out—and they won't have to go through the embarrassment of walking back to their office.

- **Make sure you have documented everything** prior to the termination. Document all the behaviors that led to termination and all the meetings and discussions you have had before you get to the point of termination.

- **If you suspect the employee may become violent**, plan to have a law enforcement professional or security guard nearby.

- **Follow your company's policies and procedures** related to termination as written in the employee handbook. Not doing so can greatly increase your risk for litigation.

- **Make sure the personnel file contains a document signed by the employee** acknowledging each disciplinary action or warning. This document should also be signed by you and another witness. If the employee files a lawsuit and it goes to trial, a credible witness can be key.

During the meeting:

- **Be straightforward.** Tell the employee you have bad news and then give the facts honestly and carefully. Do not sugarcoat the reason why you are terminating the employee.

- **Give concrete examples.** Don't simply say the employee "is not a good fit." The specific reasons for termination might be apparent from the company's records, but if you don't address these legitimate reasons during a termination meeting—or worse, makes statements inconsistent with the legitimate reasons for firing the employee—it can appear to a judge or jury that you invented after-the-fact reasons to justify the termination.

- **Be brief.** Limit the session to 10 minutes. Don't talk too much—the more you say, the more likely it is that you'll say something wrong.

- **Remind the employee about any confidentiality or non-compete agreements signed.** This will emphasize how serious you are about enforcing such agreements and will force the employee to have second thoughts about violating them.

- **Consider having the employee sign a release from legal claims.** You can offer additional severance pay in exchange. That way, if the employee's attorney contacts you regarding a possible wrongful termination suit and you're worried your documentation won't hold up in court, you'll be protected.

After the meeting:

- **Arrange for HR to take the employee after the firing.** They can explain any severance package, benefits and COBRA and answer any questions.

- **Require the employee to return confidential documents**, keys or company property at that time. Consider changing passwords and codes once the employee leaves.

- **Immediately let your other employees know about the termination.** Do not, however, give the reason for it. You want to save the employee from as much embarrassment as possible while preserving his or her privacy. It is wise to discuss with the employee in the termination meeting what will be told to co-workers and get the fired employee's agreement.

- **Be careful what you say** should potential employers inquire. A bad reference could lead to a libel suit.

Q: Do I need to tell employees why they are being fired?

A: Legally, it depends on state law. But from a practical standpoint, it's a good idea to give a reason. If you don't, the employee may look at his or her firing suspiciously and be more likely to take legal action.

Creating Solid Documentation

Let's say you terminate an underperforming employee and then later that employee sues for wrongful termination. You're in a position where you'll need good documentation as part of your company's legal defense. Would your documentation be sufficient to prove you did not act impulsively but based your decisions on legitimate reasons?

Documentation of performance issues and discussions you have with employees are not only some of the best proof you can take to court, but could discourage a lawsuit altogether. An employee's attorney may not be so quick to file a suit if the evidence is stacked against his or her client.

When you take disciplinary action against an employee, you must create and keep a good paper trail of what steps have been taken. This will include:

- Specifics of the incident or behavior that led to the disciplinary action

- Who was involved

- What happened

- When it happened

- Where it happened

- Who the witnesses were

- How the employee explained the incident

- What the supervisor said

- The circumstances surrounding your meeting with the employee

- What you said regarding your expectations about the employee's future conduct

Q: An employee is not performing and I want to fire her before she wastes any more of my time. However, I don't have any documentation.

A: You can fire her—but you may not want to. Documentation is not generally required before firing an employee. However, if the employee sues for wrongful termination, you will need documentation as your legal defense. So it pays to take the time to create it as you go through the disciplinary process. That way, you'll have it in the end should you need to fire.

Q: Can I go back and create the documentation—after the fact?

A: If you try to backdate documentation, it's usually obvious. A better approach is being honest. Write the documentation by starting with the statement, "On (date), I realized I have put off documenting ongoing problems with (employee). Here is what I remember."

Tips for creating documentation that will back you up in court:

- Use a consistent format when documenting incidents. This will show you have been fair and objective and that your actions are not the result of discrimination.

- Document everything—all the problems you had with the employee, all actions and behaviors that led to the employee's discipline.

- Include the date every incident took place.

- Notify the employee that you have placed the documentation in his or her file. Require the person to sign the paperwork to show that he or she has read it. If the employee refuses to sign, simply make a note of the fact. Then ask another manager or witness to sign that she or he has witnessed the employee's refusal.

- Get the facts right. If one error is found, there may be others. This does not help your credibility.

- Make it a habit to create disciplinary reports and other documentation promptly—not weeks or months after the fact. When documentation is created any later than that, it doesn't go over well in a courtroom.

- Make sure the employee signs and dates the document. Every piece of documentation you create should be signed by the employee and dated.

- Support your statements with facts. For example, you may write that the employee showed violent behavior. But you need to also write why you think that—for example, the employee screamed, raised a fist or lunged toward you.

- Do not write your personal notes in the margins. Never do this unless you're not worried about a judge seeing what you've written.

- Do not lie—ever. This can backfire in court.

- Enforce your policies and procedures consistently. If you discipline one employee for coming in late too often, make sure you discipline everyone else who does the same thing. Otherwise you could be accused of discrimination.

- Include specifics. Don't just write that the employee's attitude needs to improve. Write specifics—like John needs to stop complaining to other employees and stop refusing to do work he doesn't want to do.

Conducting Investigations

Over the course of your career, you will inevitably have to conduct investigations of a variety of events such as theft, accidents, safety rule violations, absenteeism or falsification of records. This may involve investigating someone's character, finances and relationships.

In general, you need to conduct an investigation when:

- An employee files a formal complaint or grievance

- An employee informally reports a questionable situation

- An employee is suspected of misconduct

- A rule, policy or law is violated

As a manager, it is your right to conduct investigations and, in many instances, your legal duty. For example, if you know—or should know—about an incident of discrimination, harassment or threat or a safety problem, you must promptly take remedial action. But to decide what that remedial action is, you may need to dig deeper into what happened and get the facts. If you fail to conduct investigations in such situations, you are likely to lose in court should an employee file a claim or lawsuit.

Some of the more important laws and legal situations that may require you to conduct investigations include:

- Job discrimination: Civil Rights Act of 1964 (Title VII), the ADA and the ADEA

- Safety and health: OSHA

- Drug-free workplace: Drug-Free Workplace Act of 1988; DOT drug testing regulations

- Background and credit checks: Required to minimize your liability for negligent hiring

ALERT: When conducting an investigation, two areas deserve your utmost care: What you ask and how you get the information.

When conducting investigations—regardless of how little experience you have—you must be fair and objective while obtaining the information that you need to resolve the issue.

Dealing with the informant:

- Thank them for speaking up and being open and assure them you will handle the information confidentially.

- Ask for a description—in their words—of what occurred.

- Request they put this information in writing.

- Follow up with them after the situation has been addressed—but don't divulge any confidential information such as what disciplinary action was taken.

Tips for conducting a legally safe investigation:

- Know when an investigation is in order—and legally required.

- Set goals for the investigation—for example, to establish whether an employee has stolen money or experienced sexual harassment.

- Move quickly to identify witnesses and documents.

- Interview all witnesses.

- Organize a list of questions to be asked of witnesses.

- Start out with general questions, and then zero in on more specific questions.

- Ask open-ended questions to encourage the witness to talk.

- Secure all files and records potentially involved.

- Maintain complete confidentiality throughout the process.

- Do not promise complete confidentiality—you may have to release names and documents to meet legal requirements—but assure witnesses you'll do your utmost to protect their privacy.

- Review every file and document.

- Visit the place where the incident occurred, if necessary.

- Stay objective and focused on the facts.

- Respect the privacy of those involved.

- Take good notes for documentation purposes.

CHAPTER 8

Handling Today's Hottest HR Issues

To excel in your position, you must not only successfully handle the day-to-day HR responsibilities of your job—the hiring, firing, disciplining, counseling, coaching and training of employees. You also must stay on top of the latest and most challenging issues—the legal hot spots—and minimize their impact on you workplace.

This section will tackle some of the hottest areas, identify the pitfalls and help you avoid trouble before it starts.

Sexual Harassment

In recent years, more and more sexual harassment cases are going before the EEOC and federal and state courts. As a result, the legal definition of sexual harassment is expanding and changing. Yet, despite widespread awareness of sexual harassment, many businesses are unsure of how to prevent the problem in their workplaces—or address the problem should someone complain.

Sexual harassment is a form of discrimination that violates Title VII of the Civil Rights Act of 1964. According to the EEOC, sexual harassment occurs "when submission to or rejection of this conduct explicitly or implicitly affects an individual's employment, unreasonably interferes with an individual's work performance or creates an intimidating, hostile or offensive work environment."

There are two kinds of sexual harassment:

1. **Hostile environment** is the most common form of sexual harassment. A hostile environment may occur when repeated behavior creates an intimidating, hostile, abusive or offensive environment. For example, a co-worker may repeatedly ask another co-worker for a date or give a co-worker a shoulder rub or comment about a co-worker's appearance in an intimidating way.

2. **Quid pro quo** (a Latin term meaning "this for that") is an easily recognizable form of sexual harassment. It occurs when a supervisor, manager or other authority figure withholds, demands and/or promises a benefit by pressuring an employee to unwelcome sexual conduct. For example, an employee who fails to submit may be denied a promotion or his or her life may be made difficult by the supervisor.

How do you know what constitutes unwelcome sexual behavior and what doesn't in your workplace? The following are examples of conduct that—if unwelcome—may be considered sexual harassment:

- Unwanted jokes and gestures
- Offensive words on clothing
- Sexual comments and repartee
- Touching
- Scratching or patting a co-worker's back

- Grabbing an employee around the waist

- Blocking an employee's ability to move

- Repeated requests for dates that are turned down

- Unwanted flirting

- Transmitting or posting e-mails or pictures of a sexual or other harassment-related nature

- Displaying sexually suggestive objects, pictures or posters

- Playing sexually suggestive music

Managers and supervisors on the front line are responsible for creating a workplace in which any form of harassment is not tolerated. You can't afford to brush off any complaint of sexual harassment. When an employee complains that he or she is experiencing sexual harassment of any type, it is your legal and ethical duty as the employer to:

- Take the complaint seriously.

- Immediately take the appropriate steps to investigate the complaint.

ALERT: The EEOC rules state that the victim's word alone may be enough if there are no witnesses.

Tips for investigating a complaint of sexual harassment:

- **Interview the employee who filed the complaint.** Gather the facts—including what happened, when, where and with whom. Determine if there were any witnesses and get their names.

- **Interview the accused employee.** Tell the person a complaint has been filed and warn the employee about the danger of retaliation. At this point, do not give the accused the name of the accuser.

- **Determine the severity of the situation.** Can your resolve it face-to-face in confidence? If so, bring the parties together and try to reach a resolution. If the complaining employee does not agree to this session or if the accused denies any wrongdoing, then you need to conduct a more in-depth investigation.

- **Interview all witnesses** and anyone else who may have knowledge of the incident. Be careful to protect the privacy of all those involved.

- **Separate the two temporarily** if the complaint is interfering with day-to-day work or if you fear the accused may retaliate or intimidate the accuser.

- **Weigh the evidence** and make a determination of whether sexual harassment has occurred.

- **Take the appropriate disciplinary action** if you determine that sexual harassment has occurred.

- **Offer the victim support** and, if necessary, restitution—for example, you may need to reverse decisions made about promotions or unjust performance appraisals.

- **Stay on guard** for any signs the accuser may retaliate.

- **Document everything.**

TIP: Make and keep complete and accurate documentation of any and every complaint of sexual harassment. If an employee is not happy with your investigation, they may take legal action.

Tips for preventing sexual harassment:

- **Regularly assess your workplace** for signs that a problem may exist so that you can take corrective action early. Look for problems like common use of sexually explicit language, the telling of off-color jokes or sexually oriented rumors.

- **Post your organization's sexual harassment policy** where everyone can see it. If your organization does not have an established policy, post the EEOC guidelines and identify specific conduct that is considered unacceptable.

- **Be firm and consistent.** Do not tolerate offensive jokes, language or comments from women or men. Immediately counsel any employee who needs to adjust their behavior.

- **Educate employees** by providing sexual harassment training and information.

- **Be a role model.** Always be gender-neutral in your attitude.

- **Be accessible** to employees and willing to hear out any complaints they may have.

- **Let employees know there are several different ways to complain.** Make sure if an employee's supervisor is the source of the complaint, there is a complaint route that bypasses that person.

- **Respond immediately**, fairly and confidentially to any complaint of sexual harassment.

T____ F____ The employee harassing another employee can be someone of the same sex.

T____ F____ The harasser can be any person connected to the employee's work environment—including the employee's boss, a customer, or a vendor or supplier.

T____ F____ Any employee who is impacted by the conduct can complain about sexual harassment. For example, if a manager is involved in a sexual relationship with an employee and treats other employees differently than his/her lover, those other staff members can claim harassment.

T____ F____ Sexual harassment can occur only if the employee can prove the behavior resulted in firing, a transfer, a salary decrease or any other action adversely affecting his or her job.

Answers: 1) True 2) True 3) True 4) False

Classifying Employees: Employee vs. Independent Contractor

Proper classification of the people who work for you—as employees or independent contractors—is a big issue that is often overlooked by managers. Determining who an independent contractor is can be complicated. There is no set-in-stone formula. The key lies in the degree or extent of the right to direct and control the person. You must examine each case carefully.

In general, if you have behavioral control and financial control, you likely have an employee in that situation.

What if you get it wrong? It could be costly. The IRS and state revenue departments are increasingly viewing independent contractors with suspicion. Any company using contract labor solely to avoid withholding and payment of payroll taxes should beware. If you misclassify an employee as an independent contractor, you may be held liable for employment taxes for that worker, which could add up to thousands in addition to other fines that may apply.

Employee: In general, anyone who performs services for you is your employee if you can control what will be done and how it will be done.

For employees, employers:

- Are responsible for the withholding and timely remittance of federal income taxes, state and local income taxes and FICA taxes from wages paid to their employees

- Owe, and must remit, their own share of payroll taxes, such as FICA and federal and state unemployment insurance, on employee wages

- Must adhere to labor laws and regulations for workers' compensation, working conditions and minimum wage laws

- Generally provide benefits such as vacations, holidays with pay, health insurance and pension and profit sharing plans

- Must report wages paid to employees and the amounts of various taxes withheld on Form W-2; in addition, Forms 940 and 941 (and perhaps others) must be filed for wages paid to employees

Independent contractor: In general, you have the right to control or direct only the result of the work done by an independent contractor, and not the means and methods of accomplishing the result.

For independent contractors, employers:

- Do not have to withhold or pay any taxes on payments to them

- Do not have to offer benefits

- Must report amounts paid on Form 1099

Q: Deciding who is and isn't an employee is confusing. Help!

A: Try following these general principles:

Behavioral Control—An employee is generally told when, where and how to do the work.

Financial Control—An independent contractor can realize a gain or loss. An employee will be paid by the company and taxes are to be collected by the employer.

Type of Relationship—Usually, independent contractors will have a written contract with specific outcomes to include a timeline.

ALERT: You can't classify workers as independent contractors but still expect to control them as employees and dictate when, where and how they work.

Determining FMLA Leave

It has been more than 10 years since the Family and Medical Leave Act (FMLA) became law. The federal law was passed to help employees balance work and family responsibilities. It allows an eligible employee to take 12 weeks of unpaid leave in any 12-month period for any of the following conditions:

- The birth of a child, adoption of a child
- The employee's serious health condition
- A family member's serious health condition

When the employee's leave is over, you must reinstate the employee to the same position the employee held before taking leave—or to a comparable position.

As a manager, you may be finding it's getting tougher—not easier—to fulfill the confusing requirements of the FMLA. What are your primary responsibilities under FMLA?

- You must determine whether the reason for the leave request is covered by the FMLA.
- You must determine whether certification of the reason for the leave will be required.
- You must determine the type and amount of paid and unpaid leave the employee may be eligible to use.
- You must provide a timely response to the leave request.
- You must notify the employee that the leave is being so designated and will be deducted time off work from the employee's remaining FMLA leave entitlement.
- You must designate FMLA covered leave on the employee's leave records.

What you need to know about FMLA leave:

- If your company has a group health plan for employees, it must also continue insurance coverage for employees on FMLA leave.
- You cannot discipline, demote or fire an employee on FMLA leave.
- You cannot count an employee's FMLA leave as an absence in violation of your company's attendance policy.

- You must allow employees to use their accrued paid leave—such as accrued paid vacation leave, personal leave or unspecified paid time off—while on unpaid FMLA leave.

- An employee also may use accrued paid sick leave—but only if the reason for the FMLA leave is covered by your company's sick leave policy or a state law.

- Employees must give 30 days' notice if the need for the leave is foreseeable. If it is not, then the employees must give whatever notice is possible and practical.

- The employee may take leave intermittently—rather than all at once. For example, an employee may need to take an afternoon off every week for chemotherapy.

- You can choose to require employees to provide medical certification that they or a family member suffers from a serious health condition. You can ask the employee for medical certification from the doctor. You also may ask for a second opinion from a doctor you choose. If the employee is absent for an extended period of time, you can require medical re-certification—but not more than once every 30 days.

- If your state has its own medical and family leave laws, you must follow whichever law—federal or state—gives the employee the most protection.

> **Q:** Do I—as an employer—have any rights under the FMLA?
> **A:** It may not seem like it. But you do. For example, you have the right to temporarily reassign an employee on intermittent or reduced-schedule leave to a position that is not negatively affected by the employee's recurring periods of leave. Let's say the employee holds a position where attendance is important—perhaps the employee answers a heavy number of phone calls. This right can work to your advantage.

Monitoring Employees

Almost every manager has—or will have at some time in the future—employees whom they suspect spend too much time surfing the Web, making personal calls or sending inappropriate e-mail. If this has happened to you, you naturally want to solve the problem and end your worries so you can get back to what's really important. Chances are, you've wondered: Can—should—you monitor your employees' telephone calls, voice mail, e-mail, Web site usage? You monitor their behavior—the way they dress, how they greet customers, the hours they work. So what's the difference?

There are valid reasons for monitoring employees' electronic behavior. In fact, recent surveys show most employers are doing some form of monitoring. Why?

- To ensure legal compliance
- To limit legal liability. You must prevent employees from being exposed to offensive graphic material, jokes and animated greeting cards—and charges of hostile work environment.
- To maintain productivity. Excessive Web surfing, personal phone calls and e-mail exchanges can eat up a tremendous amount of time.
- To protect their proprietary information. You need to know if employees are e-mailing competitors with confidential numbers, strategies, plans or other information.

It's a confusing area—one in which you must have all your ducks in a row. As an employer, you may monitor your employees' communications within reason—as long as you do not violate your employees' defined privacy rights under federal and state law. However, you need to tread carefully in these uncertain waters. Yes, you're trying to do your job and keep an eye on what your employees are up to. And you can't afford to allow employees to take advantage, blatantly misuse their time on the job—or even break the law. But you don't want to come across as overly controlling of every little thing your employees do. Where's the balance? How do you avoid a workplace in which employees operate out of fear and where productivity actually decreases rather than improves?

In other words, the question isn't whether you have the right to monitor employees—yes, you do have a legal right to monitor the work of employees using equipment that belongs to them. The question is how to go about it. Here are some guidelines:

- Establish a policy outlining the extent to which employees will be monitored. Inform employees of the policy in writing.
- Inform employees you reserve the right to monitor because they are using company-provided equipment.
- Require employees to sign a disclaimer that acknowledges your company's right to monitor.
- Don't give employees a reason to believe their communications are private. Let them know up front monitoring may be used in certain situations.
- Be reasonable when you monitor. Reserve monitoring for those instances when you have a suspicion something is wrong.

An electronic communications policy should state that:

- All computers, telephones and other electronic equipment are the property of your organization.

- You reserve the right to monitor or access all employee Internet, e-mail, computer, voicemail, and telephone usage for any business-related purpose.

- Your company prohibits sending any discriminatory, offensive or unprofessional messages via e-mail, voicemail or the Internet.

- Video cameras may be used in areas other than restrooms, locker rooms, or rooms designated for changing clothes.

- An employee who violates any part of the policy will be disciplined and possibly terminated.

Q: Am I allowed to walk up behind an employee and see what is on his or her computer terminal?

A: Yes. As long as you, as the employer, own the equipment you are free to monitor the employee using it.

Q: Can I monitor my employee's g-mail account?

A: Yes—when it's opened from a work-based computer, employers can recover and read Internet-based e-mail like g-mail and hotmail. That's because the e-mail is saved to your local, company-owned hard drive.

Workplace Violence

Workplace safety is a major problem in the United States and has become a top concern for today's managers and organizations. And increasingly, the people who handle "human resources" are the target of threats and the organization's first line defense in preventing violence from occurring.

You can't promise violence will "never happen here." Even with a high level of security in your workplace, violent incidents can and do still erupt. But you can take proactive steps to reduce the threat of violence. And—should violence occur—you can have a plan in place for responding, minimizing the situation and protecting your employees.

Tips for preventing violence:

- **Be alert to the predictors of violent behavior.** Employees who use intimidation, talk about guns and weapons, seem paranoid, complain "the company" never listens to them, express desperation, have a history of violence.

- **Do background checks when hiring.** Check for past criminal convictions, restraining orders and problems at past jobs. If you fail to investigate a potentially violent employee and the employee does become violent, you could be facing a lawsuit from the victim or victims.

- **Treat employees fairly.** Establish policies, distribute them and follow them. That way, an employee will be less likely to think you are "picking on" him or her and less likely to get angry and explode.

- **Create an anti-violence policy.** Make sure every employee is aware violence will not be tolerated and violent workers will be fired.

- **Respond immediately to any and all threats.** Don't assume an employee was "just joking around." Examine all the facts, even if you think the incident was perceived incorrectly.

- **Train employees.** They must know what is and isn't acceptable and how to respond if they are a witness to or victim of violence.

- **Secure your workplace.** Install video surveillance, appropriate lighting and alarm systems. Limit access by non-employees to your facility by using ID badges, electronic tags and security guards.

- **Limit the amount of cash on hand** by providing drop safes.

- **Give staff out in the field cell phones.** Tell them to call in daily with a work plan for where they will be.

- **Offer a security guard escort service** or police assistance at night when employees walk to the parking lot.

- **Instruct employees** to alert you to any concerns about safety, especially if an employee is yelling, shouting or threatening others.

What to do if violence occurs:

- Call 911 immediately and follow their instructions.

- Notify security in your organization.

- Move people away from the scene as quickly as possible.

- Secure the area.

- Provide prompt medical attention.

- Stay calm.

- Report the incident to the local police.

- Inform victims of their legal right to prosecute.

- Offer debriefing sessions and counseling to victims and witnesses.

- Investigate the incident and implement corrective actions.

Worksheet: Are you doing everything you can to prevent workplace violence?

Check those statements you can honestly answer "yes" to.

☐ I feel I know my employees and recognize when their behavior is out of the ordinary.

☐ When I see any predictors of violent behavior become patterns, I document them, talk to the employee, discuss the behavior in terms of the workplace, require counseling and report the behavior to the proper people in the company.

☐ My employees have been trained to report any unusual behavior to me or Human Resources.

☐ I follow our company's progressive discipline process so employees are never caught off guard by my criticism or feel they have been singled out.

☐ I always treat employees with dignity—especially when disciplining or firing them.

☐ I give the potentially violent person somewhere to turn for help.

CHAPTER 9

Where to Go for Help When You Don't Know the Answer

Stumped by a problem you're not sure how to handle? Worried an issue may blow up? Want to make sure all your ducks are in a row before making a decision? One of the big advantages of understanding the basics of HR is that you know something about employment law and can head off a lot of problems on your own. However, sometimes you may need additional help and wonder where exactly to go. There is help available …

Check With Your HR Department

Consult with your HR staff if your company has one. Treat them like you would any other consultant or expert. They can serve as a sounding board ... an early warning system ... an objective facilitator in the grievance process ... a mediator in conflicts ... and a place where you can blow off steam.

To get the most from them:

- Give them all the information they need to advise.

- Don't leave out important details related to the issue.

- Don't try to second guess them. Ask questions when you don't understand, but listen carefully as well to what they say—and, just as important, to what they don't say in an effort to preserve confidentiality.

- Check with them before paying for outside advice. But understand that in some areas they may be better equipped to provide a second opinion.

Consult With a Lawyer

From time to time, you may need to check with a lawyer to confirm your plan of action or get advice on complex legal issues. A short discussion with a lawyer can help you determine if a problem is brewing and what to do to minimize it. How often you will need a lawyer's help depends on how many employees you have, the kinds of issues you run into, how regulated your company is by the government and many other factors.

For example, it may be a good idea to ask a lawyer to review contracts, agreements, newly created policies and employee handbooks and advise you on terminations. Of course, if an employee sues you, you will need to consult with an attorney immediately.

Perhaps your company has a lawyer on staff you can consult—or an outside attorney they use. If not, find a lawyer yourself by talking to colleagues in your community—accountants or bankers, for example.

Do Your Own Research

Check out the law libraries. There may be one available to the public in your county courthouse, state capitol, a major public library or a law school. There you may find books and journals that summarize and interpret the law for you.

Check out on-line resources. Just about every federal agency related to employment law has a Web site—for example:

- U.S. Equal Employment Opportunity Commission: *www.eeoc.gov*

- U.S. Department of Labor: *www.dol.gov*

- U.S. Department of Justice: *www.usdoj.gov*

- Internal Revenue Service: *www.irs.gov*

You can also look up the Web sites related to specific laws—for example:

- Title VII of the Civil Rights Act of 1964 (Title VII): *www.eeoc.gov/abouteeo/overview_laws.html*

- Age Discrimination in Employment Act of 1967 (ADEA): *www.eeoc.gov/policy/adea.html*

- Americans with Disabilities Act of 1990 (ADA): *www.ada.gov*

- Family and Medical Leave Act: *www.dol.gov/esa/whd/fmla*

Other helpful Web sites address specific issues, such as:

- Employee privacy: *www.privacyrights.org*

- Disability rights laws: *www.disabilityinfo.gov*

- State laws: *www.statelocalgov.net*

- Workplace violence: *www.workviolence.com*

- State Labor Departments: *www.dol.gov/dol/location.htm*

Check With a Professional Association

Society for Human Resource Management: *www.shrm.org*

The premier association for members of the HR professional community, offering such services on-line as white papers on important topics, discussion, a searchable database for jobs, and special privileges for members only

American Society for Training and Development: *www.astd.org*

The world's largest association dedicated to workplace learning and performance professionals

International Personnel Management Association: *www.ipma-hr.org*

Not-for-profit, international association for public sector organizations and agencies in the human resources field

National Association of Personnel Services: *www.recruitinglife.com*

A primary resource for companies in the staffing industry including temporary, direct hire, and contract organizations worldwide.

Consult a Periodical

HR Magazine (Society for Human Resource Management): *www.shrm.org/HRmagazine*

Workforce Magazine: *www.workforce.com*